Cabbage:

Cures to Cuisine

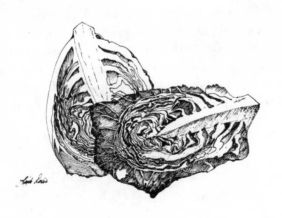

by Judith M. Hiatt

Library of Congress Cataloging in Publication Data
Hiatt, Judith M., 1950—
    Cabbage: cures to cuisine / by Judith M. Hiatt
        p.   cm.
    Includes bibliographical references.
    ISBN 0-87961-188-X : $13.95
    ISBN 0-87961-189-8 (pbk.) : $6.95
    1. Cabbage—Therapeutic use.   I. Title.
RM666.C13H53   1989
615'.323123—dc20   89-12741
                                                              CIP

Photography by B.B. Burkhart and Judith M. Hiatt.
Illustrations by Linda Hiatt Davies.

Books for a better world

Naturegraph Publishers, Inc.
P.O. Box 1075
Happy Camp, California 96039
U.S.A.

Dedicated to those who try
what others dismiss as too simple;
to those who are willing to believe.

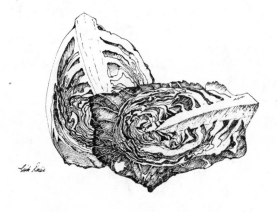

Also to ma chouchoute, *Amanda*,
wishing her a long and healthy life.

CONTENTS

Introduction—The Autobiography of a Cabbagehead   **10**
*La défense du livre. Regal associations to cabbage. Response to
the question, "Why cabbage?" Author's discovery while ill in
France of cabbage as a cure for bronchitis. Past associations with
cabbage. Favorite children's poem about fairies and cabbages.
Appreciation for cabbage enhanced by seeing the vegetable cure
the common cold, cuts, bruises, and other afflictions.*

Chapter I—Cabbage as Medicine **20**
*Brief history of the development of medicine. Use of cabbage as a
medicine by ancient Greeks and Romans, including 87 remedies
in Pliny's* Natural History. *Recent studies in the U.S. indicating
cabbage as a cancer preventive, reiterating what the Greeks and
Romans said 2000 years ago. The lack of information about
cabbage as a medicine in the United States and historical reasons
why its medicinal properties are unknown. Current popularity of
cabbage and herbology in France.*

Chapter II—Cabbage Cures for the Rat Race **27**
*Common medical complaints of modern Western societies and
ways in which cabbage can help prevent or cure them: cancer,
alcoholism, hangover, cirrhosis of the liver, colds, sore throat,
bronchitis, indigestion, ulcers, varicose veins, gangrene, scurvy.*

Chapter III—How Cabbage Works **40**
*Benefits of natural vitamins and minerals found in plants.
Correlation of vitamins and minerals found in cabbage to its
medicinal claims.*

Chapter IV—The Cabbage Patch..................... **48**
Description of botanical hierarchy: crucifer family, brassica genus (mustards, watercress, horseradish, and turnips), and the oleracea species (cabbage, broccoli, cauliflower, Brussels sprouts, collards, kale, kohlrabi). How to grow cabbages. Optimal soil and fertilizer conditions. Gardener's lore about when to plant cabbages, compatible and incompatible garden mates, etc. Common cabbage pests and simple non-toxic ways to prevent and control them. Ways to pick and store cabbage.

Chapter V—The Culinary Cabbage **69**
Complementary foods and spices to enhance the taste of cabbage. How to keep cooked cabbage from causing unpleasant odors. Cabbage recipes, both raw and cooked.

Chapter VI—Ailments and Cabbage Remedies........ **90**
Ways to prepare cabbage for medicinal use. List of ailments treated by cabbage with indications for its application.

Bibliography **115**
Index.. **122**

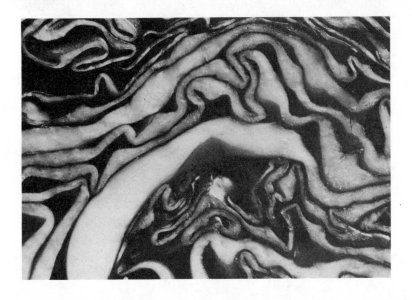

ACKNOWLEDGEMENTS

Special thanks to my good fairy, Sandy Anderson, who whispered words for my heart each time I became discouraged. Without her guidance I would never have undertaken this project; she is in every stage of the work, from its inception to completion. Kim Long, I thank, for sharing his experience on writing, publishing and marketing; David Young, for the beneficial exchange of time, talent and technology. I am equally grateful to Pat Wagner and Leif Smith, to Tom and Cissy Severance, to Dr. Bob McFarland, and to the many friends who so willingly became my guinea pigs.

Thanks to my family: to my dad, Dallas Hiatt, who passed on a love of gardening and who gave me advice about cabbage's earthly needs; to my mom, Charlotte Hiatt, for scouting out little known facts about ways to use cabbage; to my sister, Linda Hiatt Davies, whose illustrations enliven these pages and whose editing reflects the educator she is, teaching me much about writing as I created this book. Thank you's go to all the other members of my family for their constant teasing and support.

To Christiane and Maurice Netter, I am especially grateful for sharing their knowledge of medicinal plants and for the friendship and care they offered me while in France.

Most of all, I want to thank my partner and husband, Bruce Burkhart, who supported me through the on-going labor of this work. His photographic expertise was invaluable, and without his collaboration and critique, this book would have been quite different.

FOREWORD

I must say a few words of advice here about the medicinal use of cabbage. In good faith I can say that normal consumption of cabbage is very beneficial to most people. Aside from eating too much cabbage concurrent with a thyroid problem or with hypoglycemia, I have found no evidence of cabbage being harmful to one's health. As with many beneficial things, however, overindulgence can upset the balance of good health. Neither the publisher nor I will assume responsibility should you develop adverse effects from eating excessive amounts of cabbage. If you have any existing medical problems you wish to treat with cabbage, please consult your health care professional before a change in diet. Otherwise, let good common sense be your guide.

My intentions in writing this book have not been to undermine the medical profession nor to negate the importance of modern medicine in our lives. I have simply found something that has repeatedly cured me and which, when researched, seems to have cured many others before me. The testing of cabbage's medicinal powers I leave to those with more scientific resources. I have chosen instead to limit my book to the cultural use of cabbage throughout history.

Introduction

THE AUTOBIOGRAPHY OF A CABBAGEHEAD

What stands on one leg with its heart in its head? Cabbage—and yet that's only one of the many tricks of this common garden vegetable.

However far-fetched it may seem, cabbage (*Brassica oleracea capitata*) provides a highly effective natural remedy for a long list of ailments: from sore throats to bruises, ulcers to varicose veins, acne to gangrene. Known as the "poor man's medicine" in France and commonly used as a folk remedy in many countries, it is surprising that the ability of cabbage to cure a diverse number of ailments is virtually unknown in the United States. Given the renewed interest in Western societies in health and natural medicines, it seems appropriate to tell others of the gift of cabbage. Cabbage has for too long been incognito as a simple garden vegetable, but in terms of its health-giving mission, cabbage can stand on its own one leg and speak for itself.

> *"The time has come," the Walrus said,*
> *"To talk of many things:*
> *Of shoes—and ships—and sealing-wax*
> *Of cabbages—and kings."*

From Through The Looking Glass *by Lewis Carroll*

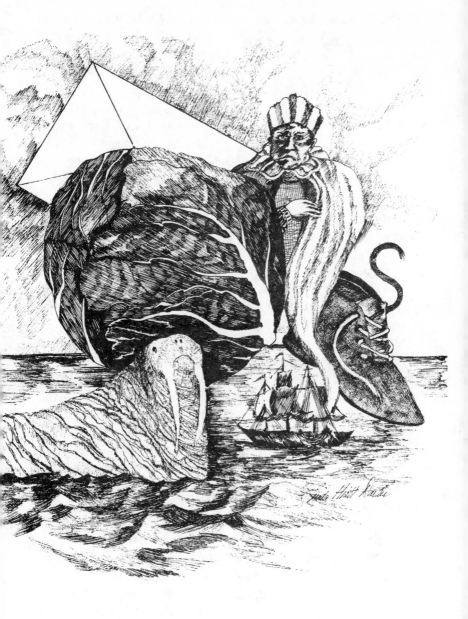

✤✤✤✤✤✤✤✤✤✤✤✤✤✤

In France, they claim that a baby boy is born under a cabbage (chou) and a baby girl under a cauliflower (choufleur).

✤✤✤✤✤✤✤✤✤✤✤✤✤✤

Somehow the idea of writing an entire book about cabbage seems surprising to most people. "A cookbook?", they usually ask. "Well, actually it's more than a collection of recipes," I tell them. "Cabbage has for centuries been thought of as a medicine, used by the ancient Greeks and Romans to combat cancer, ulcers, inflammations, infections, and as a general tonic for good health." The response is uniformly one of amazement, unless I'm talking to someone from France, China, or eastern Europe. In many countries of the world our cabbage of low esteem is highly revered.

A cabbage aficionado for some time now, if I'm called a cabbagehead I take no offense. Although in English the term means "dunce," in French it is not pejorative. "En avoir dans le chou," literally meaning to have something in your cabbage, is said of a person of intelligence. "Mon petit chou," "mon gros chou" or "chou chou" are terms reserved for especially dear people. How cabbage in the United States ever got its neglected status is a puzzle to me. Cabbage is full of good things. Humble yet strong, it gives health to those who partake of it. Therefore, when people associate me with cabbage or call me a "cabbage queen," I feel a certain sense of honor to be ranked among history's royalty.

Cabbages and Kings, and Queens, and Gods . . .

You are probably wondering how the lowly cabbage can have anything to do with kings and queens. Pick up nearly any book on vegetable gardening, and cabbage is usually called the "king of vegetables." Although the origins of that title remain obscure, one can guess it came from cabbage's ravenous need for nutrients. It takes them selfishly from the soil to the impoverishment of its neighbors, much like a feudal lord. The rose is a traditional symbol of royalty, and, by its form if not its botany, the cabbage certainly resembles a rose. Naturally, only a vegetable with a head could wear a crown, and the cabbage dynasty reigns over head lettuce hands down in food value and taste.

✤✤✤✤✤✤✤✤✤✤✤✤✤✤✤✤

Jade kale leaves were found inside the tomb of the Egyptian ruler, Akhenaton.

✤✤✤✤✤✤✤✤✤✤✤✤✤✤✤✤

Other regal associations than those exist, for throughout history cabbage and nobility have gone head in hand. Jupiter, according to the ancient Romans, was the source of this vegetable. He literally sweated cabbages into existence, plants sprouting from the drops of his perspiration as they fell to the ground. Little known is the fact that ancient Egyptians esteemed the cabbage as a sacred plant, erecting altars to its worship in their homes. During the Greek Empire, in the colony of Ionia, people swore an oath of truth upon this vegetable. "By cabbages swear I," (*per Brassicam*) is an expression that first appeared in ancient Greek literature around 500 B.C.

With such a rich background, one wonders how the cabbage came to lose its noble stature. Gone are the altars from homes and the use of cabbageheads in courts to swear in witnesses. From the king of vegetables in antiquity, time has reduced cabbage in the United States to a mere companion of corned beef. The last loyal subjects of this healing vegetable are a disbanded number of cabbage lovers, and they're only loyal to its taste. Since people often ask, not without amazement, how I ever chose the topic of cabbage for a book, I will include a little personal history to explain its significance to me.

Why Cabbage?

It is far easier and safer to prevent illness by the observance of the laws of health than to set about curing illness which has been brought on by our own ignorance and carelessness.
—Mohandas Gandhi

Several years ago while working in Europe I traveled to southern France to visit friends. All sorts of mishaps befell me en route, not the least of which was missing train connections and deciding to hitchhike instead. That proved to be a costly mistake, as I spent long hours in the rain followed by a night in the Gare de Lyons, with no place to sleep but the cold cement floor (they somehow had overlooked courtesy benches in that particular train station). As misfortune would have it, rides became scarce while the drizzle continued the next day. I developed a drizzle of my own which promptly turned into a severe case of bronchitis and accompanying head cold.

When at last I arrived in Aix en Provence, my friends went promptly to work. Being very knowledgeable about medicinal plants, homeopathy, and other natural cures, they had an extensive library of herbal texts. After consulting several, they made me fresh cabbage juice with instructions to gargle and swallow it. To my amazement, the cabbage instantly relieved the raw pain of my sore throat.

The cabbage juice was not, however, a modern miracle drug to mask the symptoms of my illness; the pain started to reoccur after just a few hours. Three or four times a day they repeated the treatment. They tucked me into bed each night encased in a cabbage poultice: layers of crushed raw leaves over my chest and throat to relieve the congestion and absorb toxins through my skin. Had I not been so miserable, my rational side would surely have dominated, and I'd have politely declined this bizarre vegetable treatment. But my friends acted with such authority, and I was so in need of being pampered, that I gave them no resistance. By the end of the week my bronchitis was cured—a most impressive feat, since minor sore throats I had before then generally lasted twice as long.

Thus began my adoration of cabbage, not unlike the zealous ardor of a religious fanatic for a new-found faith. I discovered that instead of waiting until my sore throat was in full force, I could stop it in its initial stages by drinking fresh cabbage juice. What a discovery!—the answer to the common cold! Thereafter, I tried to win converts to my "religion," citing the worship of cabbage

❖❖❖❖❖❖❖❖❖❖❖❖❖❖❖

*A cabbage
is a cabbage
is a rose.*

❖❖❖❖❖❖❖❖❖❖❖❖❖❖❖

as a sacred plant by both the ancient Egyptians and Greeks. I spewed out facts about cabbage's medicinal abilities, proclaiming it a healer at least of the rank of Oral Roberts. Misty-eyed, I raved over the beauty of the cabbage rose as one would speak of a lover. (A friend once told me, "Lucky the man you would love as much as cabbage.") Little by little my circle of converts grew. The believers were those who tried cabbage for sore throats, bruises, or hemorrhoids and found that it worked.

It is, indeed, hard to keep the momentum of a faith going, especially in the face of heavy skepticism. Of that I encountered plenty in my attempts to cure the ills of friends and family. For many it seemed laborious to chop

✤✤✤✤✤✤✤✤✤✤✤✤✤✤✤✤

Cabbage was such an important vegetable in Europe prior to the discovery of the Americas because there were fewer vegetables available then. Tomatoes, corn, potatoes, squash, beans, and peppers all came from the new world.

✤✤✤✤✤✤✤✤✤✤✤✤✤✤✤✤

and blend cabbage when it's so easy to take a cold capsule or run off to the doctor for an office call and prescription. They were missing the beautiful simplicity of using cabbage to avoid costly illnesses and expensive medical treatment requiring loss of work. Preparing cabbage means taking a little more time in the short run to avoid losing time and money in the long run.

From those who disliked the taste of cabbage, I could accept rejection. Perhaps others were offended when I remarked, "How wonderful that you have hemorrhoids/ulcers/indigestion/varicose veins!"—happy to have guinea pigs upon whom to test the touted remedies. Whatever their reasons, I hope seeing this book in print will help reverse their hesitations about cabbage. Those who were willing to try gave me the encouragement to continue working. Their positive results validated the many claims that cabbage works and helped keep my momentum and faith going.

In Remembrance of Things Past

Once I envisioned writing a book, past associations with cabbage came flooding back to me. My grandmother was very dear to me. She used to write poetry and I could remember several of her poems with animated garden vegetables, primarily the cabbage. She wrote in a neat and tidy style, with verses rhyming. Her favorite poet was James Whitcomb Riley, and she used to read us many of his poems written for children. Full of goblins and ghosts and witches, his poems were a vivid part of my childhood. Vaguely I recalled and later found one of Riley's poems,

"Bud's Fairy Tale," in which the way to fairyland was via the cabbage patch. At least according to some European folklore, fairies mount cabbage stalks like witches ride brooms. In this excerpt a fairy directs Bud to follow:

> "Come on!" he says; an' went a-limpin' 'long
> The garden-paph—an' limpin' 'long an' 'long
> Tel—purty soon he come on 'long to where's
> A grea'-big cabbage-leaf. An he stoop down
> An' say, "Come on inunder here wiv me!"
> So I stoop down an' crawl inunder there,
> Like he say.
>
> An' inunder there's a grea'-
> Big clod, they is—a' awful grea'-big clod!
> An' nen he says, "Woll this-here clod away!"
> An' so I woll' the clod away. An' nen
> It's all wet, where the dew'z inunder where
> The clod wuz—An' nen the Fairy he
> Git on the wet-place: Nen he say to me,
> "Git on the wet-place, too!" An' nen he say,
> "Now hold yer breff an' shet yer eyes!" he says,
> "Tel I say Squinchy-winchy!" Nen he say—
> Somepin' in Dutch, I guess.—An' nen I felt
> Like we-'uz sinkin' down—an'sinkin' down!—
> Tel purty soon the little Fairy weach
> An' pinch my nose an' yell at me an' say,
> "Squinchy-winchy! Look wherever you please!"
> Nen when I looked—Oh! they 'uz purtiest place
> Down there you ever saw in all the World!
>
> —James Whitcomb Riley

In my heady state of remembrance, the past reappeared before my eyes. I remembered the tears I had shed one summer, overwhelmed by the beauty of the cabbage I was cutting. My job, working in a German restaurant, was to prepare *rotkohl,* a cooked red cabbage dish. By far my favorite task, I looked forward to the times when I could wash and core the cabbageheads. Using a large slicer, I stood back and marveled at the delicate lace doilies of red cabbage falling into the bowl. I told no one of my infatuation with cabbage, sure others would not understand.

This book is primarily about cabbage (the original, wild kind) and its offspring, head cabbage, which first appeared in the Middle Ages. Ancient folklore, legends, and proverbs passed down for centuries say nothing of broccoli or Brussels sprouts, relative latecomers to the cabbage family. Nutritionally similar, cauliflower or broccoli could be substituted for cabbage in the remedies, though I admit I have not tried it. It would be rather uncomfortable to wear a poultice of cauliflower on one's chest at night or a tedious bother to peel and roll each miniature leaf of a Brussels sprout.

♣♣♣♣♣♣♣♣♣♣♣♣♣♣♣♣♣♣♣♣♣♣♣♣♣♣♣♣♣♣♣♣♣♣♣♣

The Ten Commandments contain 297 words; Lincoln's famous Gettysburg Address, 266 words; the writers of the Declaration of Independence used a mere 300 words; but the government DPS order to regulate the price of cabbage contains 26,911 words!

♣♣♣♣♣♣♣♣♣♣♣♣♣♣♣♣♣♣♣♣♣♣♣♣♣♣♣♣♣♣♣♣♣♣♣♣

Kale and collards, on the other hand, have broad leaves similar to those of the cabbage. They can be rolled and applied easily to the skin, hence they should work as effectively as cabbage at healing, perhaps even better. Kale and collards are the darling prince and princess of the cabbage dynasty, having surpassed head cabbage in their quantity of many vitamins and minerals. Rightfully, this book should encompass them all—not only cabbage but also kale, collards, kohlrabi, broccoli, brussels sprouts, and cauliflower. To do so would have required writing at least another volume, so I have let cabbage—the most well known of the vegetables—represent the entire family. Substitute as you like.

❖❖❖❖❖❖❖❖❖❖❖❖❖❖❖

Luther Burbank, the renowned hybridizer of plants, tried to hybridize cabbage but found that nature had already transformed it into broccoli, cauliflower, kohlrabi and Brussel sprouts, and he could take it no further, but instead ended up with something similar to the wild cabbage.

❖❖❖❖❖❖❖❖❖❖❖❖❖❖❖

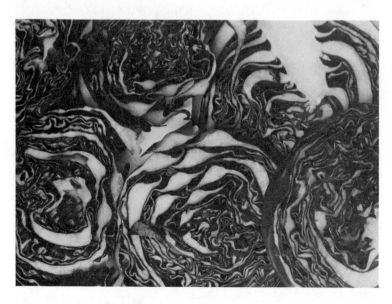

Chapter I

CABBAGE AS MEDICINE

We must not be embarrassed to borrow from the people that which is useful to the art of healing.
— Hippocrates

The history of cabbage parallels the history of herbology, the oldest form of medical treatment. Man's first attempts to cure physical problems came about after much observation of the natural world. Constantly exposed to the environment, he became aware of and sensitive to the plants and animals around him; in fact, that sensitivity was a necessity for survival. He surely noticed and imitated the way some animals ate specific plants when they were ill. Today, we know that cats and dogs eat grass to provoke vomiting if they have eaten something toxic, sheep eat yarrow for relief from poisons, and before giving birth female elk instinctively gnaw on aspen bark, a natural pain killer and anesthetic. Specific animals in each given habitat must have done much the same, surviving on those plants which produced a therapeutic effect on them. What animals seem to have known by instinct, man has had to develop using his intellect, and it has been a slow and tedious process.

As humans became less nomadic and settled in a particular region, they began to purposefully cultivate plants for food and healing. Those early gardens were truly the first pharmacies. Over centuries people gathered knowledge based on identification and experimentation about herbs and their powers of healing. Not only did they note specific plants but also which parts—roots, leaves or flowers—were the most beneficial. They determined at what time of day, during which season and under what phase of the moon the plants should be gathered for maximum potency. Those who survived taught their young

❖❖❖❖❖❖❖❖❖❖❖❖❖❖❖

On the Isle of Jersey, England, they make walking sticks out of wild cabbage stalks which often grow twelve feet tall. Canes made from these stalks were also prized in British hospitals, being both strong and flexible.

❖❖❖❖❖❖❖❖❖❖❖❖❖❖❖

what they knew about healing practices, and medical knowledge passed from generation to generation by word of mouth.

Small communities began to form in which usually one man or woman became the healer, entrusted with guarding and dispensing herbal remedies. These shamen and other healers would often spice their roots and leaves with doses of ritual and magic. To pass on the tradition of medicine within that tribe, they wisely chose a successor worthy of learning their plant secrets. As commerce developed among different groups, travelers exchanged seeds and traded fresh and dried herbs. Thus, the sphere of influence of local medicinal plants expanded.

The wild cabbage, native to western France and southwestern England, was among the most prominent of the first domesticated plants. It was first cultivated over 4000 years ago. Cabbage's area of cultivation eventually extended into Europe due to the Celts, a tribe occupying those regions along both sides of the English Channel.

The Celts sacked Rome in 387 B.C. In that day and age an invasion lasted months or even years. Warriors had to travel on foot or were, at best, stationed at a remote camp for extended periods of time. They needed to plan for food and medicine, so they took cabbage seeds or plants along

❖❖❖❖❖❖❖❖❖❖❖❖❖❖❖❖

Jacques Cartier first trans-
ported cabbages to North
America from Europe in
1541-42 on his third voyage.

❖❖❖❖❖❖❖❖❖❖❖❖❖❖❖❖

for both purposes. Upon conquering the new lands, they forced the local people to adopt their own customs and grow food that they were accustomed to eating. In such a manner the Celts introduced cabbage into new territory to the south and east principally the entire Mediterranean area that we know today as southern France, Italy, Greece, Yugoslavia, Turkey, and Egypt.

Although there are Chinese, Indian and Egyptian herbal texts dating from 2900 B.C., written records of cabbage as a medicine did not appear until the Greco-Roman era (500 B.C. to 400 A.D.). Greek authors such as Hippocrates, Chrysippus, and Theophrastus wrote treatises on medicine and were the first to extensively document cabbage as a healing agent of importance. Hippocrates, often called the father of medicine, is given credit for founding wholistic medicine, having held the belief that the body can heal itself if it is in balance. He recommended cabbage for diseases of the kidneys, for dysentery and poisoning by fungi, as well as for increasing the amount of milk in nursing mothers and regulating menstrual discharge.

Chrysippus, a scholar credited with over 750 works, wrote an entire volume on the ability of cabbage to heal all parts of the body. Dioscorides, a Greek physician from Asia Minor who attended to the soldiers of Nero's armies, wrote the authoritative work *De Materia Medica,* a model herbal for centuries thereafter for its practical and extensive coverage of medicinal plants. This work lists tame and wild cabbage as a remedy for a host of ailments from dim eyesight to snake bites. In a work entitled *Inquiry Into Plants,* written over 24 centuries ago, Theophrastus classified existing herbs. He mentions three kinds of

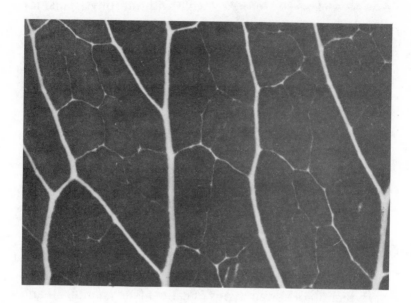

Cabbage veins detail.

cabbages: curly-leaved, smooth-leaved, and wild. Philistion advised treating snake bites, gout, ulcers, and hiccups with cabbage, while Epicharmus thought it to be an effective remedy for diseases of the testes and genitals, for fevers and maladies of the stomach and for bites of the shrew-mouse. Equally, Dieuches and Pythagoras wrote in praise of the medicinal virtures of cabbage in reference to healing various parts of the body.

Romans, such as Pliny the Elder who wrote *Natural History* in the first century A.D., elaborated upon the earlier works by the Greeks. Pliny praised the cabbage highly, listing it for 87 remedies (compared to garlic's 61). The Greeks and Romans used cabbage primarily as medicine rather than as food. Cato the Elder, also known as Cato the Censor and author of *De re rustica,* especially hated physicians. He treated nearly everything with a prescription of *Brassica oleracea,* stating that the Romans had lived very

❧❧❧❧❧❧❧❧❧❧❧❧❧❧❧❧❧
Greek proverb: "In the far-
off field, the cabbages are
fine." (The grass is always
greener on the other side of
the fence.)
❧❧❧❧❧❧❧❧❧❧❧❧❧❧❧❧❧

well without physicians for over 600 years thanks to the use of cabbage. Based on its prominence as a healing plant among the ancient Greeks and Romans, and with the expansion of both their empires, the influence of cabbage as a medicine grew.

In the seat of two of the greatest civilizations in history, cabbage was a virtual panacea, reportedly able to cure many of the known diseases of that time. According to Cato, cancer was only curable by means of cabbage. Believed to be a viable cure for cancer by both the Greeks and Romans, recent evidence suggests that the ancients were perhaps not so far from the truth. Research shows a link between raw cabbage in the diet and the prevention or reduction of certain types of cancer (see chapters II and VI). More extensive research is currently in progress to determine whether this cancer-preventive benefit of cabbage is true. What is true, however, is that somewhere along the course of history we lost information about many of cabbage's healing properties.

The main cause of this loss was due to a decline in the Middle Ages in the use of plants as medicine. Discoveries in chemistry heightened expectations for miraculous new cures to man's afflictions. By then, Europe was already witnessing the union of commerce and pharmacology. Herbal cures were spurned by the growing class of physicians, since they could obtain no profit from them. Indeed, they viewed traditional herbalists as quacks eager to deprive them of their near-exclusive hold on the medical profession. Apothecaries could make more money selling mysterious compounds rather than prescribing what grew in everyone's garden. Thus, single plants thought to have healing properties were no longer in vogue; physicians preferred costly prescriptions which included an array of exotic elements. If the prescriptions did include plants, there were often so many in the compounds that the medicinal value of each individual herb was hard to determine. Cabbage, chamomile, yarrow, and garlic gave way to ground rhinoceros horn, goat's hooves, pulverized pearls, cayenne, and a host of hard-to-get and expensive ingredients.

❖❖❖❖❖❖❖❖❖❖❖❖❖❖❖❖

Cabbage ranked fourth as a favorite vegetable in 1967 in the United States, after potatoes, lettuce, and tomatoes. It tends to be consumed more in rural areas than in cities and more in lower rather than higher income areas.

❖❖❖❖❖❖❖❖❖❖❖❖❖❖❖❖

Monks, however, continued to perform a valuable service for herbology by planting medicinal herbs in their gardens for healing the poor. The peasants, therefore, learned natural healing remedies using plants. In that way herbal medicine continued its predominantly oral tradition through the 12th century, while the new medicine, aided by advances in chemistry, seemed more modern, and became the fashionable form of treatment in all of Europe.

Herbal and modern scientific treatments could have coexisted to the benefit of humankind, the one in the role of prevention and the other curative; however, the successes of the new medicine during the Middle Ages overshadowed traditional and simpler ways of healing. Herbalism, like many other forms of medical treatment (homeopathy, chiropractic, bonesetting, etc.), was associated with the common folk and heid in disregard by those of the wealthier classes.

However, in some parts of the world cabbage's medicinal virtues have withstood the passage of time. Today the Chinese are in the forefront for preserving traditional herbal remedies. In present-day France, where traditions are not easily forsaken, herbology is still a popular form of medical treatment, within which cabbage holds a place of prominence. It may be that much of its esteem in France is a holdover from earlier times when France was part of the Roman Empire. Regardless of the reasons, numerous French texts praise cabbage as a major healing substance. As cabbage spread as a vegetable throughout Europe, Asia, and the Americas, some of the knowledge of its medicinal uses went along with it. Cabbage is included in a number of modern European, Chinese, Russian, and Latin American herbals, as well as in the ancient texts, for healing a diversity of human ailments.

Red cabbage, crosscut.

Chapter II

CABBAGE CURES FOR THE RAT RACE

*Where a cure can be obtained by diet, use no drugs,
and avoid complex remedies where simple ones will
suffice.*   —Rhazes, Arab physician (865–925)

Noise pollution, high-speed living, and contamination
of our bodies with improper foods and toxic substances
take their toll on our physical, mental, and spiritual well-
being. The most common medical complaints of those in
the rat race are related to a fast-paced, mechanized lifestyle. Below are afflictions to modern man that cabbage
can help treat. Instructions for preparing cabbage to
prevent specific illnesses are found in the section
"Ailments and Cabbage Remedies," pages 90–114.

Cancer

Although we tend to think of cancer as a 20th-century
scourge afflicting industrial-based societies, this disease
has been a health problem since antiquity, having been
listed in medical texts during the Roman era. It may be,
however, that cancer is on the increase in Western
societies today due to the stressful conditions of our
existence. Studies have indicated that the higher the stress
factor in one's life, the greater the risk of getting cancer.
We are not totally vulnerable to the random onslaught of

this disease, however. In large part we help or hinder our bodies to ward off illness by what we choose to eat. Research has linked dietary habits to both the prevention and the spread of cancerous cells in the body.

Nearly 2000 years ago, Cato declared that carcinoma was incurable by any other means than the treatment of cabbage. He was perhaps not so far from the truth. A study compiled by the National Academy of Sciences, entitled *Diet, Nutrition and Cancer* (1982), surveys major international reports on the prevention of cancer. The study states that "by some estimates 90% of all cancers in humans are influenced by environmental factors including diet." Examples are drawn from different racial groups, such as blacks and Japanese in the United States who do not have the same cancers as black Africans or Japanese, respectively, but do get the same cancers as other Americans. That indicates that the environment, more than race or genetic heritage, influences our predisposition to cancer.

Findings indicate that certain types of cancer seem to be prevented by including natural sources of fiber and vitamins A and C in the diet. Cabbage and its related family members—broccoli, cauliflower, and brussels sprouts—are the only vegetables specifically named throughout the N.A.S. study, and are high in fiber and vitamins A and C.

The committee believes that there is sufficient epidemiological evidence to suggest that consumption of certain vegetables, especially carotene-rich (i.e., dark green and deep yellow) vegetables and cruciferous vegetables (e.g., cabbage, broccoli, cauliflower, and brussels sprouts), is associated with a reduction in the incidence of cancer at several sites in humans. A number of nonnutritive and nutritive compounds that are present in these vegetables also inhibit carcinogenesis in laboratory animals. (Diet, Nutrition and Cancer, p. 1-11)

Several of the individual studies that were surveyed reported that the risk of cancer decreased when raw fruits and vegetables, especially cabbage and its related family members, were eaten on a regular basis. The cancer cases showing the most protective effect from the cruciferous vegetables were gastric, colon, and rectal cancers. In studies conducted in Japan, New York and Minnesota, the greater the consumption of raw foods high in fiber, the lower the incidence of cancers of the colon and rectum. According to the N.A.S. study, the fiber in cabbage may help flush carcinogens through the intestines, decreasing the time they are in contact with tissue, thereby not allowing them to stagnate and grow in the body.

❖❖❖❖❖❖❖❖❖❖❖❖❖❖❖❖
Cabbage was once such an important food in Scotland that every meal included kale soup. Soup, in general, and the pot it is cooked in has come to be called "kail."
❖❖❖❖❖❖❖❖❖❖❖❖❖❖❖❖

Preliminary research indicates that cabbage also contains a substance which inhibits the formation of cancerous cells in the body. Synthetic vitamin supplements do not provide this protective ability and the study recommends obtaining vitamins through food in its raw state. The fresher the food, the higher the natural vitamin content, so those who grow cabbage, kale, cauliflower, broccoli, brussels sprouts, or collards in their garden or who can be assured they are getting wholesome, untreated vegetables, may have a jump on the development of cancer. There is no guarantee that by eating cabbage a person will not get cancer, but the study indicates that the risk is significantly reduced.

In *Life Extension: A Practical Scientific Approach* (1982), authors Durk Pearson and Sandy Shaw report that cabbage and cauliflower are said to have properties, labeled indoles, that deactivate bodily toxins and carcinogens.

These vegetables also stimulate an oxidase enzyme system in the liver that inhibits the formation of cancer-causing chemicals in the body. The book goes on to state that cabbage and cauliflower also prevent carcinogenic activation in the body of PAH, polycyclic aromatic hydrocarbons. PAH are produced when something is smoked or burned, for example cigarettes or charcoal-broiled meats. Although not carcinogens themselves, PAH are thought to cause 40–80 percent of human cancers. Eating cabbage regularly can interfere with the formation of cancerous cells that otherwise might develop when burned substances are ingested.

There is still much research to be conducted in the area of cabbage and cancer prevention. Currently the American Institute for Cancer Research is funding studies for cancer prevention through cabbage extracts. Eating raw cabbage regularly seems to provide some health insurance against getting cancer, especially of the colon, rectum, intestines, or esophagus.

Alcoholism, Hangover, and Cirrhosis of the Liver

Since alcohol is a legal drug in our society, we suffer widely from its effects. At the end of each workday, many of us come to depend on that drink to help forget problems and stress. When stress increases, often so does our desire for alcohol. A hangover is just a temporary reminder of the toxins we have drunk, while prolonged use leads to alcoholism, a major dependency on alcoholic beverages that can eventually cause the liver to deteriorate to the point of cirrhosis, when it ceases to function well.

Cabbage as a remedy for the ill effects of wine has been around since antiquity. The Greeks and Romans relied heavily on the cabbage plant to offset their overindulgences in alcohol. Cato said, "If you wish to drink much at a banquet, before dinner dip cabbage in some vinegar and eat as much as you like. After dining eat five leaves. The cabbage will make you as fit as if you had had nothing, and you can drink as much as you will." Aristotle, likewise, recommended the same before a big feast.

There is an old Greek legend that implies that cabbage is a counteractant to wine. Lycurgus, the prince of Trace, had the most highly esteemed vineyard in all the land, except for the grapes produced by his neighbor, Dionysus, the god of wine. Jealous of his rival's grapes, Lycurgus disguised himself in peasant's clothes and stole into the neighboring vineyard to destroy its vines. He was caught cutting down the last plant, and for punishment he was tied up with one of his own grapevines and ridiculed by all who passed. In humiliation he wept, and as his tears fell to the ground they turned into cabbages.

On a purely botanical level this same opposition between cabbage and the vine can be seen. Grapevines

♣♣♣♣♣♣♣♣♣♣♣♣♣♣♣♣♣

According to German folk-lore, the Man in the Moon was banished there as punishment for stealing a cabbage on Christmas Eve.

♣♣♣♣♣♣♣♣♣♣♣♣♣♣♣♣♣

❖❖❖❖❖❖❖❖❖❖❖❖❖❖❖

In Denmark, the cabbage has been a prominent vegetable since the times of the Vikings. Kitchen gardens came to be known as cabbage gardens, since cabbages were so generally grown.

❖❖❖❖❖❖❖❖❖❖❖❖❖❖❖

will coil around most every plant but grow in the opposite direction of the cabbage. To the Greeks this was further evidence of the curative powers of cabbage in treating the aftereffects of wine.

Mattioli, a 17th century Italian physician, stated that cabbage would remove all the effects of drinking too much wine if eaten at the end of the meal.

In Alsace, France, as well as in bordering German provinces, sauerkraut juice is taken for reducing the effects of too much alcohol. Yugoslavians drink the juice of pickled red cabbage for their hangovers.

The Irish traditionally eat cabbage on New Year's Day. Given the custom of celebrating New Year's Eve by drinking excessively, one wonders if the cabbage tradition did not evolve out of a medicinal necessity to soothe the woes of a hangover.

Colds, Sore Throat, and Bronchitis

The common cold with its characteristic sore throat is a modern curse. Millions of dollars are spent each year in the elusive search for its cure. Often it develops into the more severe state of bronchitis. Our highly air conditioned or overheated homes contribute to weakened respiratory passages, and pollution from industry and auto exhaust inflicts further damage. Unless we are in excellent health, we are often unable to resist the onset of a cold.

Based on my experience, cabbage is one of the best therapeutic measures for warding off colds. It is important to eat raw cabbage or gargle and drink fresh cabbage juice at the first indications of a cold: sore throat, stuffiness, or feverish and achy feeling. Our bodies are constantly giving off signals as to our state of health—we must only be more in tune to those messages. By recognizing and acting upon them, it is possible to stop the development of many physical ailments.

For an already existing cold or sore throat, cabbage treatment will help relieve the pain and will speed up recovery, but keep in mind that cabbage's strength is *prevention.* Thanks to cabbage, I've only had a few winter colds or sore throats in years. I eat cabbage in some form as soon as I begin to feel sick, but before the cold gets established. This is most remarkable because before my "cabbage days" I used to get three or four colds accompanied with a sore throat each winter. Eating raw cabbage on a regular basis is the best preventive measure I have found for colds.

One Mexican natural remedy book advises smearing a mixture of pork lard, coffee grounds, and rose oil on three cabbage leaves and then bandaging one around the throat and one on the sole of each foot. While one probably

Savoy leaves, reverse side.

✿✿✿✿✿✿✿✿✿✿✿✿✿✿✿

*Beethoven's Violin Concerto
in D Minor was based on a
German folktune entitled
"Beets and Cabbages Make
Me Fart."*

✿✿✿✿✿✿✿✿✿✿✿✿✿✿✿

wouldn't want to hop into bed wearing this messy remedy, there may be some validity to its application on the soles of the feet. Many European texts advise binding herbal remedies to the soles of the feet and modern wholistic medicine includes foot reflexology as a viable form of treating illness. Reflexology recognizes the feet as surface receptors to organs and all areas of the body.

Indigestion and Ulcers

Indigestion is a consequence of our abundant living, where overeating, rather than starvation, is a primary concern. Often the pace of our lifestyle reflects the type of foods we tend to consume: fast or junk food, highly processed and preserved. When we do dine well, it usually means we eat several courses, for we think a meal is not complete without a salad, bread, soup, vegetable, main course, dessert, and often an alcoholic drink or three. No wonder we suffer from indigestion! Combine such over-indulgences with the inability to handle stress and the perfect conditions for ulcers exist. Cabbage has been proven to help neutralize the acid/alkaline imbalance of indigestion and ulcers.

While pregnant, I found that cabbage worked effectively to eliminate the heartburn I occasionally got as a natural consequence of gastric juices pushing up into the esophagus. I just ate 2 or 3 fresh leaves each time and the heartburn went away.

Pat is a friend who loves to eat spicy foods, even knowing he will suffer from indigestion. He used to take several commercially prepared medicines for heartburn, acid indigestion, and upset stomach each night. After trying cabbage juice, he found he could substitute it for the

❖❖❖❖❖❖❖❖❖❖❖❖❖❖❖❖

One pound of cabbage will yield six 2-ounce portions of coleslaw or about 5 firmly packed cups of shredded vegetable.

❖❖❖❖❖❖❖❖❖❖❖❖❖❖❖❖

synthetic remedies he had been using. To prepare his cabbage medicine he used a blender, put one cabbage leaf into it with a cup of water and drank the entire pureed liquid. He now does this before going to bed at night and has not had to eliminate any favorite foods—garlic, onions, chilies, and hot, spicy dishes—from his diet. The best part of the story is that he no longer needs any of the commerical medicines he used to buy!

One of the few widely known medicinal uses of cabbage in the United States is its ability to cure ulcers. Rural midwesterners often know to eat sauerkraut or drink sauerkraut juice to eliminate ulcers. Russians use a similar remedy for ulcers. They drink 4 to 5 glasses of fresh cabbage juice daily for one week.

Based on studies done with guinea pigs that had histimin-induced ulcers, it was found that a diet of raw cabbage cured their ulcers. From this research and other studies conducted by the U.S. Army during World War II, it was deduced that there was some factor in raw cabbage that was successful in preventing ulcers and in curing them once they had developed.

In the late 40s and early 50s, Dr. G. Cheney, of the Department of Medicine at Stanford University conducted further experiments with cabbage juice given to hospitalized ulcer patients. Of the 13 patients tested, 7 had duodenal and 6 had gastric ulcers. Each was given a quart of fresh cabbage juice each day but was able to eat a regular diet including coffee. In 11 of the 13 cases, the pain subsided in two to five days after beginning treatment. The lesions of the ulcers completely disappeared in 6 to 9 days, as shown by the daily x-rays. Only 2 of the patients required a longer treatment time, 14 and 23 days respectively, making an average healing time of 9 days for all 13 patients. Patients in the control group, consisting of 62 cases of duodenal and 6 of gastric ulcers, were cured by the traditional method of a bland diet, antacids, and anti-spasmodics in an average time of 37 and 42 days respectively.

Dr. William Shive, Professor of Chemistry at the University of Texas at Austin, performed further work with cabbage by extracting from it a substance called glutamine which he used to treat ulcers. His studies dealt with measuring the time it took for the glutamine to heal both duodenal and peptic ulcers. The results of the study showed that the ulcers of half the patients healed in two weeks. By the time of the second x-ray examination two weeks later, 83% of all the ulcers treated with glutamine were healed. These results were two times faster than for the control group given a placebo. Although Shive's findings were not as spectacular as Cheney's, both studies indicated positive results in the treatment of ulcers with cabbage.

The anti-pepsin factor in raw cabbage has unofficially been labeled vitamin U. Despite its lack of official recognition, it is an effective substance in protecting the digestive tract from pepsin, an enzyme secreted in the stomach which aids digestion. Cheney's study found that frozen cabbage juice retains its vitamin U content for up to three weeks. When cabbage is cooked or dried, however, the vitamin U is lost.

Varicose Veins and Gangrene

As a result of the popularity of the automobile in the United States, we do not walk as much as our forefathers. Further industrialization and mechanization have meant less and less physical labor on the job. Passive leisure activities, like watching sports on TV, often replace the

desire to be active and par-
ticipate in sports or outdoor
activities. Problems of circulation, such as varicose veins,
become more widespread in
people who sit at a desk all
day and get little exercise.

In France, there are documented cases where the ap-

✤✤✤✤✤✤✤✤✤✤✤✤✤✤✤✤✤

*Cabbage is the birthday
plant for the 19th of Sep-
tember, symbolizing profit
and gain. It is the emblem of
both the self-willed and the
vegetating.*

✤✤✤✤✤✤✤✤✤✤✤✤✤✤✤✤✤

plication of cabbage has reduced the swelling of the
varicose veins and eliminated the need to surgically
remove them. Applied externally on the area, cabbage
activates circulation, revitalizes tissues, and absorbs
impurities which block capillaries.

Gangrene, where body tissues actually decay due to
lack of blood to an area, is a step more serious than
varicose veins. Gangrene is not the common medical crisis
it once was. Usually, accident victims with damaged limbs
can be quickly transported to a hospital for emergency
treatment. Where amputation used to be the standard way
of treating gangrene, today it is possible to restore circulation to the area if medical help is available soon enough.
Gangrene, however, can still be a serious threat when the
person is not able to receive immediate attention.
Cabbage can help promote circulation to the damaged
tissue in such cases, while waiting for professional help.

One French medicinal plant book gives numerous
case histories showing how amputation was avoided by
applying dressings of cabbage leaves to the damaged
limbs. Around 1880 a case was documented in which the
driver of a cart fell from his seat and was run over by one of
the wheels. The damage was severe enough to warrant
amputation, the most common treatment at that time to
arrest the spread of gangrene. A local priest advised the
victim's mother to dress the leg with crushed cabbage
leaves. By the time the doctor arrived, the patient could

move his leg and there was both a significant return of color as well as a reduction of the swelling. With continual applications of cabbage leaves, the man was able to walk and resume his activities within 8 days.

In a similar case in 1875, a seventy-five year old man in France was afflicted with gangrene of the artery on the inside half of his right leg and foot, resulting in blackened skin. By wrapping the leg and foot with crushed cabbage leaves the man's skin changed color from black to brown to red and showed signs of improvement within three weeks.

Dioscorides was quoted as saying, "Being beaten and mixed with honey, they (cabbages) are good against irritating gangrene."

Scurvy

Scurvy can hardly be considered an affliction of the rat race but it is, nonetheless, a common disease worldwide in areas where fresh sources of vitamin C are not available. It is thanks to cabbage that scurvy is no longer a major health threat in some northern European areas which do not have access to imported citrus and tropical fruits throughout the winter months.

In 17th century France, common belief held that only the touch of a king could heal those afflicted with scurvy. Voltaire reported a case in which a man with scurvy sought out his king in order to rid himself of the disease. The king's touch did not do the trick. Cabbage, however, often called the king of vegetables, was known by some at that time as a cure for scurvy. Unfortunately, the man went after the wrong king.

Captain Cook sailed around the world in three separate voyages in the latter half of the 18th century. During this period scurvy was still a rampant disease not only among sailors but on land as well. During his second expedition in command of 118 men on the *Resolution*, Cook recorded the following observations on antiscorbutic foods:

Sour Krout, of which we had also a large provision, is not only a wholesome vegetable food, but, in my judgement, highly antiscorbutic, and spoils not by keeping. A pound of it was served to each man, when at sea, twice a week, or oftener when it was thought necessary... These, Sire, were the methods, under the care of Providence, by which the Resolution performed a voyage of three years and eighteen days, through all the climates from 52 degrees North to 71 degrees South, with the loss of one man only by disease, and who died of a complicated and lingering illness, without any mixture of scurvy.

With the Russian exploration of the Bering Strait in the early 1700s, shiploads of Russian sailors spent years searching for land, only to find frozen terrain much like Siberia's. These first Russian immigrants found they were developing scurvy yet they would not try the Eskimo cure of eating raw animal organs. Instead, after traveling to Russia with furs, they returned with the seeds of two plants to ward off scurvy: cabbage and rhubarb.

✤✤✤✤✤✤✤✤✤✤✤✤✤✤✤✤✤✤✤✤✤✤✤✤✤✤✤✤✤✤✤✤✤✤✤✤✤

Some pioneers made their fortune during the California Gold Rush in 1849 not by discovering gold, but by growing and selling cabbage, rich in vitamin C, to the miners suffering from scurvy.

✤✤✤✤✤✤✤✤✤✤✤✤✤✤✤✤✤✤✤✤✤✤✤✤✤✤✤✤✤✤✤✤✤✤✤✤✤

Chapter III

HOW CABBAGE WORKS

Some set more by such things as come from a distance, but I rec'lect mother always used to maintain that folks was meant to be doctored with the stuff that grew right about 'em. —Sarah Orne Jewett
American writer (1849-1909)

Prior to 1940 cabbage consumption in the United States was high: statistically each person consumed about 15 to 20 pounds a year. Before the second World War it was hard to buy oranges, lemons, and other citrus fruits, unless one happened to live in California or Florida. Folks elsewhere had to get their ration of vitamin C from fruits and vegetables grown closer to home. That often meant relying on cabbage, a major supplier of vitamin C.

Unlike many other garden crops, cabbage can be counted on to survive the first two or three frosts. Even in cool northern states it tends to be available fresh until late fall. Cabbage is also one vegetable that stores well over the long winter months. Studies done by the U.S. Department of Agriculture show that cabbage retains 75% of its vitamin C even after two months of proper cold storage. These factors and the general accessibility of cabbage helped to make it a staple in most American homes in the first half of this century. The U.S.D.A. estimated that by 1966, however, with daily air-freight shipments of fruits and vegetables from around the

world, the amount of cab-
bage eaten a year per capita
was only 9 pounds, greatly
reduced in two and a half
decades.

Let's face it. Compared
to such exotics as mangos,
papayas, pineapples or kiwi
fruit, cabbage may seem plain

❖❖❖❖❖❖❖❖❖❖❖❖❖❖❖❖

*Spanish proverb: "He who
likes cabbage, will like its
outer leaves." (If you like
someone, you will also like
that person's friends and
family.)*

❖❖❖❖❖❖❖❖❖❖❖❖❖❖❖

and uninspiring, especially after years of the same dull
recipes (see new recipes in Chapter V). When one thinks
of a good source of vitamin C, it is usually not cabbage that
comes to mind, although by weight it contains as much
vitamin C as orange juice. Not only does cabbage have
ample quantities of vitamin C, but it's also loaded with
other vitamins and minerals: vitamins A, B-6, K and U,
calcium, magnesium, potassium, phosphorus, and iron.

A lot of information about the health benefits of
vitamin C has led us to believe it's the single most important nutrient we need in order to be well. In actuality,
every vitamin and mineral has its purpose, and often that
purpose is interconnected. Vitamin C, for example, strengthens blood vessels, promotes healthy teeth, gums, and
bones, increases the absorption of iron in the blood, helps
resist infection, and aids in the production of collagen, a
fibrous protein which connects tissues. For maximum
assimilation of vitamin C in the body, it must coexist with
something called bioflavonoids. Calcium and magnesium,
as well as vitamins A, the B complex, D, and E, help vitamin
C work at its best. Calcium and magnesium also pair
together to maintain healthy bones, teeth, nerves, and
muscles, and aid vitamins B-6 and D, and minerals
phosphorus, iron, and manganese. The list goes on and on.

After many years of dissecting nutrition into isolated
nutrients, we are learning that the interaction of all the
available vitamins and minerals determines the healthful

benefits, not one or two synthesized and taken alone. In *The Aquarian Conspiracy,* author Marilyn Ferguson expresses the nature of parts in relation to the whole:

> ... *each variable in any system interacts with the other variables so thoroughly that cause and effect cannot be separated. A single variable can be both cause and effect. Reality will not be still. And it cannot be taken apart! You cannot understand a cell, a rat, a brain structure, a family, or a culture if you isolate it from its context. "Relationship is everything."*

In nutrition the relationship of vitamins and minerals to each other is symbiotic. In isolation they cannot work as well. Nutrients provide us with maximum health benefits when they co-exist and interact. They do that best and most simply in fresh, natural foods—the fresher the better—from which we can get all the basic nutritional elements we need.

That's where the beauty of cabbage comes in. In its fresh, raw state it has a dozen nutrients which work together for healthy effects. Its healing qualities cannot be explained by its vitamin C alone. There are many other foods with as high, if not higher, content of vitamin C. My guess is that the medicinal workings of cabbage rely on the balance of all its nutrients and the way they interact with each other in the body. I, for one, am unconvinced of the need to take vitamin and mineral supplements to promote health when natural supplies are found in foods like cabbage for a fraction of the cost. I believe the vitamin C in cabbage to be far superior to that of a capsule of processed C, because fresh cabbage also contains bioflavonoids, vitamin B-6, calcium, magnesium, phosphorus, and iron, all of which enhance the utilization of vitamin C in the body.

A Cabbage Leaf A Day Keeps The Doctor Away

The following is a list of the major nutrients found in raw cabbage. Along with each vitamin or mineral, there is a description of how it aids the body and the corresponding claims of cabbage's medicinal properties.

Vitamin A is a fat-soluble vitamin. This means it is stored in the body rather than the excess being excreted daily as with water-soluble vitamins. For proper absorption in the body, fat-soluble vitamins must be accompanied by some fat in the diet. Vitamin A contributes to healthy skin, nails, teeth, bones, and blood. It strengthens vision, especially at night, and aids the linings of various organs like kidneys, bladder, intestines, lungs, and mucous membranes. Vitamin A helps balance thyroid deficiencies related to goiter and may help substantiate the claims that cabbage remedies goiter as well as skin disorders, colds, bronchitis, asthma, allergies, cough, sinisitis, gastritis, and diarrhea.

The Recommended Daily Allowance (RDA) of vitamin A is 400–700 retinol equivalents for children, 800 for women, 1000 for men and pregnant women, 1200 for nursing mothers.

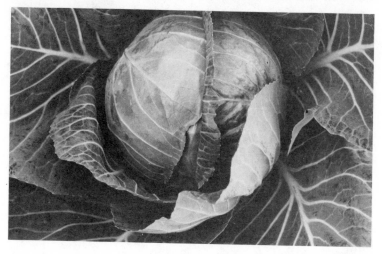

Green cabbage.

One cup of shredded savoy cabbage provides 140 IU (international units, now being replaced by the term "retinol equivalents"). That equates to 20–30% RDA for children, about 17% for women, 14% for men and pregnant women, and about 12% for nursing mothers.

Vitamin B-6 (Pyridoxine) is a water-soluble vitamin, easily destroyed by heat, sunlight, and oxidation. B-6 is available in raw cabbage and the cabbage family. B-6 is necessary for carbohydrate–fat–protein metabolism; for proper fluid retention and weight control; for good healthy skin, nerves, and muscles; for antibody formation; and for digestion. B-6 in cabbage may be responsible for its claims of treating acne and other skin problems, hemorrhoids, ulcers and digestive tract disorders, and protecting against infections. Vitamin B-6 is given to alcoholics as a nutritional supplement to aid in combating their addiction to alcohol. This vitamin in cabbage may help reduce the effects of alcohol in the body, both before and after drinking.

The RDA for vitamin B-6 for children is between 1.0 and 1.6 mg, for adults from 1.6 to 2.2 mg, and for pregnant and nursing women from 2.5 to 2.6 mg.

Vitamin C is another water-soluble vitamin. When referred to in its complex natural form, it is called bioflavonoids, composed of citrin, hesperidin, quercetin, and rutin; the synthetic form carries the label ascorbic acid. The bioflavonoids are sometimes known as vitamin P. Exposure to sunlight, heat, and oxidation will also destroy much vitamin C. Vitamin C is said to remedy infections, ulcers, allergies, arthritis, gastrointestinal disorders, scurvy, snake and insect bites, liver problems, wounds, and diarrhea, all purportedly treated by cabbage. In the form of bioflavonoids, vitamin C strengthens capillaries and is useful for treating high blood pressure. It could be a reason why cabbage aids in healing varicose veins and bleeding gums.

The RDA of vitamin C for children is 35–45 mg, for

adults 50–60 mg, for pregnant and nursing women, 70–80 mg. One cup of shredded red cabbage contains 43 mg of vitamin C, or 100% RDA for children, 72–86% for adults, 54–61% for pregnant and nursing women.

✤✤✤✤✤✤✤✤✤✤✤✤✤✤✤✤✤

Vitamin K was discovered in 1934 by a Danish scientist named H. Dam. He noticed that hemorrhaging chickens stopped bleeding after being given cabbage.

✤✤✤✤✤✤✤✤✤✤✤✤✤✤✤✤✤

Vitamin K, a fat-soluble vitamin, was named K for the Danish word "koagulation," as this element helps normal blood to coagulate. Vitamin K is found in high quantities in cabbage leaves and kale. Vitamin K can help prevent miscarriage, and can lessen menstrual flow and cramps. Vitamin K is given to mothers in labor and to babies at birth to prevent cerebral palsy. Newborn babies have temporarily low levels of vitamin K. Perhaps the age-old practice of giving cabbage to women in labor and nursing mothers helps balance the vitamin K level in the newborn. No RDA has been established for vitamin K.

Vitamin U, an anti-pepsin factor, is found principally in raw cabbage and family. Pepsin is an enzyme secreted in the stomach which aids digestion. When too much pepsin is produced, it reacts with other gastric juices and eats away at the mucous membranes of the stomach, creating an ulcer. Vitamin U is referred to in several medical journals as a vitamin, although I have yet to see it given that official label. The ulcer-fighting element does exist, regardless of its status. The high amount of vitamin U in cabbage may be responsible for cabbage's ability to heal ulcers.

As no official listing of vitamin U exists, there is no RDA available for this anti-pepsin factor. I found no studies measuring the specific vitamin U content in cabbage.

Calcium (Ca) is the most abundant mineral in the body, accounting for 2 to 3 pounds of body weight, most of

❖❖❖❖❖❖❖❖❖❖❖❖❖❖❖❖
*Cabbage is more
than 90% water.*
❖❖❖❖❖❖❖❖❖❖❖❖❖❖❖❖

which is in the bones and teeth. Aside from aiding the formation of healthy bones and teeth, calcium is necessary in the body for transmitting nerve impulses, regulating muscle contractions, helping to clot blood and maintaining cellular structure.

The RDA of calcium for adults, both men and women, and children is 800 mg; pregnant and nursing women and adolescents need 1200 mg.

Savoy cabbage has the greatest amount of calcium, 47 mg per one cup of shredded vegetable. The percentage RDA of calcium supplied by a serving of cabbage is 6% for children and adults, 4% for adolescents and pregnant and nursing women.

Phosphorus (P), like calcium, is present in the body in large amounts, mostly in the bones and teeth. It prepares the way for calcium to collect in these structural areas of the body. Phosphorus is necessary for proper breakdown of food into nutrients that the cells can assimilate. It also acts as an agent to maintain the acidity of the body and is a component in the nucleic acids DNA and RNA. Phosphorus promotes cell growth and repair which may contribute to the claims that cabbage heals wounds and bruises.

The RDA for phosphorus is identical to that of calcium at 800 mg for children and adults, and 1200 for adolescents. A one cup serving of raw shredded savoy cabbage contains 38 mg of phosphorus or about 5% recommended daily allowance for children and adults, and 3% for adolescents.

Magnesium (Mg) is stored principally in the body's bones with a smaller amount in the muscles. It is necessary for healthy functioning of the nerves and muscles. A deficiency of magnesium in the diet can cause nervousness, neuromuscular disorders, kidney problems, depression, and irritability.

The RDA of magnesium for children is 150–250 mg, 300 mg for women, 350 mg for men and 450 mg for pregnant and nursing women. A one cup serving of raw shredded cabbage contains 14 mg magnesium, or 6–9% RDA for children, 5% for women, 4 % for men and 3% for pregnant and nursing women.

Potassium (K) works hand in hand with sodium to maintain a balance of fluids in the body. Potassium is linked to healthy functioning of the heart and muscles in general and to proper electrical impulses in the nervous system. Potassium also helps metabolism of protein and carbohydrates.

There is no RDA established for potassium but rather an "estimated safe and adequate daily dietary intake" of 550–4500 mg for children (age 1–18) and 1875–5625 mg for adults. One cup of raw shredded savoy cabbage

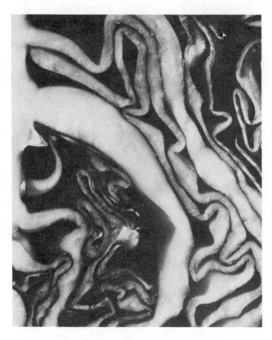

Red cabbage, cross-cut.

✤✤✤✤✤✤✤✤✤✤✤✤✤✤✤✤✤

Green cabbage is slightly richer in nutrients than red or white. The darker, outer green leaves contain more vitamin A, iron and calcium.

✤✤✤✤✤✤✤✤✤✤✤✤✤✤✤✤✤

contains 195 mg, or 5 to 35% potassium for children and between 4 and 10% for adults. Excessive amounts of some minerals can be toxic so it is not advised to exceed the range of safe quantities.

Iron (Fe) is what keeps us from being anemic, which is synonymous with listless, weak, pallid, sickly. Without an abundant amount of iron, the body's red blood cell count is insufficient. Iron is necessary for the formation of hemoglobin, located in the bone marrow, and myoglobin, present in the muscles, both of which transport oxygen to the cells and muscles respectively. Iron is a significant factor in the synthesis of collagen, which helps connective tissues heal, in the formation of antibodies, in the cleansing of the liver, in the resistance of the body to stress and disease, and in providing the body with energy. The iron in cabbage may contribute to its ability to heal wounds and to maintain a healthy liver.

RDA of iron is 10 mg for children and men, and 18 mg for adolescents and women, including pregnant and nursing women. Red and savoy cabbage contain the highest amounts of iron, .6 mg per cup shredded, or 6% iron for men and children and 3% for all others. One cup of canned sauerkraut has twice that amount of iron.

✤✤✤✤✤✤✤✤✤✤✤✤✤✤✤✤

The English word "cabbage" is derived from the French term, "caboche," meaning a head.

✤✤✤✤✤✤✤✤✤✤✤✤✤✤✤✤

Chapter IV

THE CABBAGE PATCH

Oh thrice and four times happy those who plant
cabbages! —*Rabelais*

Cabbage, broccoli, cauliflower, Brussels sprouts, kohl-rabi, collards, kale, and chinese cabbage are all from the same family: *Brassica*, if you go by the Latin name. Brassica, in correct botanical terms, is not really a family, but rather the larger grouping called a genus. It includes mustard, rutabagas, and turnips as well as cabbage and its offspring.

The wild cabbage plant, also called "sea crambe," is quite a bit like kale and collards today. The Latin name for them is *Brassica oleracea* (meaning to smell, from the Latin word "oler") *acephala* (meaning they do not form a head). Head cabbage, *Brassica oleracea capitata* (forming a head) is actually a large bud with leaves that enfold a seed case, while Brussels sprouts, *B. oleracea gemmifera*, are lots of small buds that grow up the stalk of the plant, one at each adjoining leaf.

Cauliflower and broccoli are not really flowers, as they appear to be, but "curds," or tight bunches of buds. Both are designated by the term *Brassica oleracea botrytis*, which means a "cluster." Kohlrobi, *B. oleracea caulo-rapa*, happened sometime around the 16th century. It comes from the German words"kohl" (cabbage) and "rube" (turnip) because its stem bulges out like a turnip. The group of

❖❖❖❖❖❖❖❖❖❖❖❖❖❖❖
Where did Mr. McGregor
find Peter Rabbit? Why, in
the cabbage patch, of course!
❖❖❖❖❖❖❖❖❖❖❖❖❖❖❖

Chinese cabbages are more in line with the mustards, having the names *Brassica pekinensis* and *B. chinensis.* They are cousins to the cabbage clan.

Another common name for the cabbage group is cole crops. Cole in English sounds like "cold" or "cool," and that is a good reminder about how they grow best: plenty of sunshine and fertilizer, but not too much hot weather. Cabbage is one crop that should be planted early for growth during the cool days and crisp nights of spring. If set in the ground too late, it may bolt during summer's extreme heat, not forming a head. Cabbage can also be planted past the period of intense summer heat to produce a fall crop, since it can still be harvested after several frosts. In fact, its flavor greatly improves after the temperature dips below freezing a few times. Frost makes cabbage's natural sugar content increase and it then becomes much sweeter with less of that peppery tang common to all in the mustard family.

Preparing the Soil

As soon as the ground is sufficiently thawed to be turned over with a shovel, preparation of the soil can begin. The roots of cabbage plants grow to a depth of about 12 inches, so the soil should be broken up at least a foot deep. Cabbages do best in loose soil with good drainage and that means loosened with the shovel several times.

Dried manure is wonderful for the cabbage patch, but should be worked into the soil at least a month or two before planting seeds. "Hot" fresh manure can burn tender seedlings. Pliny the Elder of ancient Rome recommended "asses' dung" but urban gardeners may have to settle for mixed peat and manure available at gardening stores.

Applying compost from last fall's leaves and the winter's accumulation of kitchen plant wastes will help produce healthy cabbages with lovely, large heads. The better the soil, the healthier the cabbages, and the more likely they will be able to resist infestation by harmful insects.

In the absence of compost or animal droppings (of the vegetarian variety, so not cat or dog, of course) a commercial fertilizer high in potash and nitrogen is essential. Packaged fertilizers provide three important ingredients to plant growth: nitrogen (N), phosphorous (P) and potassium (K), always written in that order. Potash is a potassium compound. The ratio of these minerals is listed numerically on the package, 10-10-10, or 5-5-10. Choose a product that has higher first and last numbers: 10-5-10, for example.

Seedlings can be started at the same time the soil is prepared. The young plants will be ready to transplant 6 to 8 weeks later when the fertilizer has worked into the soil sufficiently. Cabbage is variable: either an early, a mid-season, or a late crop. Check seed packages to determine the appropriate planting time. By starting several different varieties of cabbages with varying lengths of maturity, the cabbage heads will form at staggered intervals throughout the growing season. Bugs and insects that are harmful to cabbages tend to be more prolific in the early months when spring rains create ideal moist conditions for their growth. In poor soil (scarcity of earthworms is a good indicator) or in a humid climate where bugs are abundant, it might be best to wait until mid or late summer to plant a later crop.

Two-Headed Cabbages

I prefer to plant my cabbages early and get two harvests from the same plant. This is achieved by cutting the first head before it gets too big, leaving at least 4 or 5 large broad leaves around the bottom of the stalk. Within a

❖❖❖❖❖❖❖❖❖❖❖❖❖❖❖❖

Cabbage did not form a head until after the time of Charlemagne, in the 9th century. Until then it was more like kale and collards.

❖❖❖❖❖❖❖❖❖❖❖❖❖❖❖❖

few days small buds begin growing out at the base of each leaf. By being persistent and breaking off all but one (they will stop sprouting after a week or so), the resulting sprout will grow into a second, medium-size cabbage. Allowing two sprouts to grow will produce two smaller heads. Once the new heads are established, break off the former leaves. Often these miniature vegetables are the perfect amount of cabbage for one dish.

Early varieties of *Brassica oleracea capitata* can either be sown directly in the garden or begun a few weeks earlier in a protected indoor environment in individual pots. It is mind boggling to choose from the hundreds of varieties available through seed companies. A few of the standards are listed here.

Cabbage Varieties

I usually like to have several red cabbages, a few different green ones and a lot of savoy. Chinese cabbages are also fun to grow in the garden but don't hold up as well as the others when it gets hot. It is important to remember to rotate the cabbage patch each year to avoid attacks by the usual pests. In fact, it's recommended to not plant any cole crops where others have been over the last three years.

Ruby Ball is wonderful to behold, like a convoluted purple brain. The taste is mild and it stores well. Ruby Ball is an early red cabbage that produces a small, firm head in about 68 days.

Red Acre is another good red cabbage variety producing a deep purple, globe-shaped head in about 76 days.

Early Jersey Wakefield is a good one to grow, although

a favorite of rabbits. My father grows 2 each of 10 different varieties of cabbage in his garden. Throughout the summer the rabbits munch only on Early Jersey Wakefield,

✤✤✤✤✤✤✤✤✤✤✤✤✤✤
*The freezing point of
cabbage is 30.4°F.*
✤✤✤✤✤✤✤✤✤✤✤✤✤✤

ignoring the rest of the cabbages. By sacrificing two heads, Dad saves the other eighteen. Not only is he content but the rabbits are healthy, too. This variety matures quickly in 63 days and has a tender, sweet taste. Each head only weighs about 2 to 3 pounds, so the head stores easily in the refrigerator.

Early Round Dutch takes a few days longer, 72, to form large 4 to 5 pound heads that are round and compact. They have been hybridized to prevent splitting and bolting, or going to seed, so may grow successfully during hot weather.

Copenhagen Market is a popular cabbage to grow for slaws and sauerkraut. It should be planted in mid-season for a harvest in 72 days. Heads are firm and round, about 4 to 4½ pounds.

Savoy Ace Hybrid forms a large compact head about 8 inches across and 7 inches deep. It is easy to grow and does well in both heat and frost. Planting to harvest time on this variety is 85 days. Savoy's crinkled leaves are the most attractive to use in slaws and in cabbage rolls.

Savoy King Hybrid produces beautiful dark green crinkled leaves around a semi-flat head which can weigh up to about 4 pounds. I always wonder if the semi-flat types weren't cross-bred to fit in a standard refrigerator, being just tall enough to squeeze in between shelves. Savoy King Hybrid matures in 80 to 90 days and, as it is resistant to heat, it is a good one for a double harvest.

Michihli is the most common variety of Chinese cabbage. It produces a head that ressembles both celery and savoy cabbage, with thick juicy stalks topped by small crinkled leaves. Its taste is mild and sweet. Seventy days is the growing season for this one, but gardeners should get an early start while the weather is cool. If not sown in early spring, the seeds should be planted a couple of months before the first expected frost in the fall. Mature size is about 18 inches tall and 3 to 4 inches thick.

Sprouting Seeds Indoors

Have on hand: sterile potting soil; small peat pots, one per plant desired; seeds; water spray bottle; an aluminum or teflon cake pan; light from the sun or grow lamps.

Use small individual peat pots which disintegrate once planted in the soil. Fill to 1½ inches from the top with soil. Place 4 or 5 seeds, spaced evenly apart, in each pot. Cover with ¼ to ½ inch of soil, then gently pack it down. Mist the soil until damp and place each pot in the pan containing water. There should be just enough water for it to be absorbed completely by the pots with none left over in the pan. If the pots still look dry add more water. Place the pan in a warm spot with no temperature fluctuation, especially not in direct sunlight or near a heat vent.

When the seedlings first sprout, put the pan in an indirectly well-lighted spot. Keep the sprouted plants constantly damp. Do this by adding water to the pan when the seedlings appear dry and occasionally misting them with the spray bottle. When the plants grow two true leaves (after the initial dicotyledon pair), pull up all the plants except the biggest and healthiest in each pot. If the stems appear long and spindly, pack additional soil around them. This method gives one seedling per pot without having to transplant them to individual containers. After 4 or 5 weeks they will be ready to harden off.

Hardening Off

Cole crops are hardy vegetables and even when not hardened off they will probably survive, although the shock of transplanting and the exposure to outside will most likely stunt their growth. However, taking the time to gradually introduce them to the sun, wind, and cool air will ensure healthier plants. Start the process 10 days before moving them into the ground. Withhold water a few days before moving the plants outdoors for the first time. Find a protected place out of direct sunlight and wind. Move the pan outside for a few hours the first day, gradually increasing the length of exposure to 8 to 12 hours a day. Water plants in the evening after moving them indoors. After five such days they are ready to be left out overnight, barring the threat of a frost. Do this at least three nights. At this point they can be safely transplanted without trauma.

How To Plant Cabbages

Je veux que la mort me trouve plantant mes choux.
—Montaigne

Although Montaigne wanted death to find him planting his cabbages, you needn't fear the fatal touch when you plant your own.

Soil being ready and the seedlings being big enough to transplant, next determine the dimensions of the cabbage patch by figuring the number of plants and size of each. The closer the spacing of the cabbages, the smaller the

❖❖❖❖❖❖❖❖❖❖❖❖❖❖❖❖

American farmers grow about 2 billion pounds of cabbage a year.

❖❖❖❖❖❖❖❖❖❖❖❖❖❖❖❖

resulting heads. If you want to compete for a spot in the *Guiness Book of World Records* for the largest cabbage ever grown, allow the cabbages plenty of room. My personal recommendation is to forget growing the big guys (40—50 pounds in the norm is the Matanuska Valley in Alaska) and opt for pulling fewer weeds and having smaller cabbages that can be more easily stored by planting seedlings closer together.

Maximize a small plot by spacing plants diagonally. In the first row plant cabbages 12—15 inches apart. Move over 12—15 inches for the second row but offset it by planting a cabbage halfway between two in the first row. Line up the third row with the first, and so on. There will be weeds early on that try to crowd out the vegetables, but once the cabbages fill out they'll shade the ground and the weeding will be minimal.

Needed are: a spade, seedlings, fertilizer, water.

After marking where the individual plants should go, dig an 8—10 inch hole and put some compost or fertilizer in the bottom. Cover each hole with 4—5 inches of soil and then water well. Water each peat pot before setting it in the hole. Break off the bottom set of leaves and place the cabbage plant in the hole so the surface level is just above where the leaves were. That portion of stem will develop into roots. Add soil to the ground level and pack it down. Water the seedling immediately since this is a crucial time for its survival.

Don't transplant in the heat of the day. Late afternoon is the best time when the hot sun is not so direct. Once the plants are in the ground they will need water regularly, about one inch per week. In a humid climate where there's plenty of spring rain, watering is not a problem. In drier climates, check to see how deep the moist soil goes. There should be 3—4 inches of dampness. The ideal way to water cabbages is not with a sprinkler system that drops water onto the plants but by watering from the soil down. The drip irrigation method gives the roots plenty of water but keeps the leaves dry. Some insects thrive in the damp pockets of wet leaves, so only watering the soil will help control pests.

Some gardners can't really choose the optimal time for planting seeds. Weekends and holidays usually dictate when that occurs. No matter when we set aside time to plant, the weather may not cooperate. It may be raining non-stop during a convenient three-day weekend or snowing during the best time to plant by the moon. Does that mean plants will not live if these designated times are missed? Not at all, providing they are cared for in other ways.

Love as a Determinant in Plant Growth

Gigantic cabbages are a phenomenon in several parts of the world: the Matanuska valley in Alaska and Findhorn in Scotland. In the case of Alaska, cool temperatures, excellent soil and extra hours of daylight can account for the gargantuan vegetables produced. At Findhorn, where the soil was so barren others claimed nothing could grow there, founders of this garden community have attracted international attention for the agricultural wonders they have been able to perform. Love, they claim, is an essential ingredient in their success.

Jean-Jacques Rousseau, in defining the word "vegetable" for a dictionary of botanical terms, called it an "organic body endowed with life and deprived of feeling." In a letter to his cousin he wrote:

> *They will not let me off with that definition, I know. People want minerals to live, vegetables to feel, and even formless matter to be imbued with feeling.*

Although that may be so according to modern physics, I have never been able, nor will I ever be able to express the ideas of other people, when these ideas do not coincide with mine. I have often seen a dead tree which I previously saw alive, but the death of a stone is an idea which would never enter my head. I see delicate feeling in my dog, but I have never noticed any in a cabbage. (Rousseau, p. 154)

Little did Rousseau know, as he compiled his dictionary in the late 18th century, that research two centuries later would suggest cabbages, and indeed all plants, do have delicate feelings. In the 1960s, a series of experiments using a lie-detector resulted in the seeming discovery of something akin to sensitivity in plants. Cleve Backster, a former employee of the CIA and a national expert in the field of lie-detectors, wondered if he could determine the time it took his common house plant to react to its daily dose of water. He hooked the plant up to the polygraph machine, which in theory should register greater conductivity as water spread through the plant to the attached area, to monitor the precise moment when water reached that leaf.

Backster was profoundly shaken when he read the graph: The plant showed the strongest reaction, not when he watered the plant or liquid reached the leaves, but when he *decided* to give it water. Likewise, a threat to touch flame to the leaf gave the most violent reaction on the polygraph chart when he envisioned fire in his mind, less so when he actually burned the plant and not at all when he faked it. It appeared his plant instantaneously perceived his own thought processes and intentions, in a manner much like E.S.P.

Offshoots to the original lie-detector discovery included tests with music and human interaction. Talking and singing to one's plants were not uncommon practices in the late 60s and early 70s. Research indicated that plants responded favorably to rhythmic, melodic, and soft music like that of Ravi Shankar. The leaves grew toward the source of music. Hard rock music caused plants to recoil from the speakers over a period of a few weeks.

The outcome of other studies suggested love to be an important element affecting a plant's growth. Wishing plants well and telling them how lovely they are can be a dose of psychic fertilizer. Of course, water and sunlight are also essential, but human care is an important element as well. Dr. Blondel, professor of natural science at Blake

Savoy cabbage leaves.

❖❖❖❖❖❖❖❖❖❖❖❖❖❖❖

In former times in Scotland, young girls would walk blindfolded through the cabbage patch on Halloween and pull up a cabbage stalk. The size of the stalk was supposed to indicate the height and shape of the man she would marry, and the taste of it, bitter or sweet, was an indicator of his disposition.

❖❖❖❖❖❖❖❖❖❖❖❖❖❖❖

College in San Diego, determined that certain plants, such as tomatoes, potatoes, and cabbages, are more susceptible to human kindness and flattery. Just as children grow best in a climate of real love and affection, plants respond equally to someone who feeds and cares for them out of love.

Cabbage Companions

A love/hate relationship also exists between cabbage and many of its garden mates. There are some things that naturally thrive next to cabbage and that seem to promote the health of cabbage, too. Other plants do not fare well at all in proximity to any *Brassicas.* Gardener's lore over the years has come up with the following list of compatible mates:

Marigolds are commonly thought to be a natural pesticide, having an odor that is undesirable to many of the insects that harm cabbages. A few interspersed among the cabbage patch can help keep unwanted pests away. Watch out to make sure they don't take over for they're very prolific and spread quickly.

Thyme is a beneficial herb to grow alongside cabbages for repelling the cabbage worm. **Geraniums** help cabbages in the same manner.

Chamomile, also known as the garden physician, is a natural doctor among plants. When sown next to cabbages, it improves their growth and flavor. Use chamomile sparingly, about 1 plant per 15 square feet.

Mint improves both the flavor and the health of the cabbage. It also inhibits the infestation of cabbage worm butterflies and helps keep aphids away.

Sage, rosemary, hyssop, and **southernwood** are said to deter the cabbage moth, whose larvae eat the tender leaves of the plants. Hyssop seeds should be sown in the fall for early germination in the spring.

Other aromatic plants that have many blossoms are usually good to plant in the vicinity of cabbage. **Dill** not only complements the taste of cabbage in recipes but enhances its health while growing.

Rhubarb grown nearby can have a beneficial effect on cabbages. It is said to be a deterant of clubfoot, a disease which causes the plants to turn yellow and wilt. A stalk or two of rhubarb buried in the cabbage bed should help to control that disease.

Pennyroyal planted among cabbages may help curb cabbage maggots.

Celery helps control the white cabbage butterfly.

Mustard planted near cabbages is reported to attract harmful insects by a special oil it secretes. Pests are drawn to this decoy and away from cabbage.

Nasturtiums have a similar positive effect on cole crops. They improve the health and flavor of neighboring plants by drawing aphids to them. Lime can then be sprinkled on and around the nasturtiums to kill the aphids.

Hemp *(Cannabis sativa)*, or **marijuana,** was used in Holland in the 1800s as a border around the cabbage patch to repel white cabbage butterflies. Hemp is a natural plant insecticide, excreting a volatile substance that inhibits the growth of certain harmful micro-organisms.

Before the days of detergents, knowledgeable housewives and gardeners threw their soapy **dishwater,** particularly if it had soda in it, on vegetable and flower beds. This was especially beneficial to cabbages. Sour milk or **buttermilk** is also said to help cabbages when sprinkled on and around them.

DON'T Plant Cabbages Next To . . .

Strawberries. The strawberry patch is the loser.

Grapevines. Cabbages and grapevines just don't get along side by side. The grape's tendrils naturally grow in the opposite direction of a cabbage and will never coil around its stalk. To the ancient Greeks that was botanical evidence supporting the use of cabbage to counteract the ill effects of wine.

Rue. It has a harmful effect on cabbages.

Tomatoes and **pole beans.** They will not do well near the cabbage patch.

Mulching

Once the crop is planted and growing nicely, there are only a couple of things to do other than water. Mulching is useful to keep the soil cool once the weather gets hot. Ground moisture is retained longer with a covering of mulch which means it may not be necessary to water as often. Mulch can be straw, grass clippings, leaves, or even shredded newspaper that is spread around the base of each plant, several inches thick. Weeds have a harder time growing through this thick layer so mulching is beneficial for cutting down on laborious hours of pulling weeds. One disadvantage to mulching, however, is that pests often thrive in the damp

❖❖❖❖❖❖❖❖❖❖❖❖❖❖❖❖
Dutch proverb: "To go like cabbage." (To go according to schedule.)
❖❖❖❖❖❖❖❖❖❖❖❖❖❖❖❖

❖❖❖❖❖❖❖❖❖❖❖❖❖❖❖❖
French Proverb: "To answer someone cabbage for cabbage" (to answer someone pat).
❖❖❖❖❖❖❖❖❖❖❖❖❖❖❖❖

organic material and may breed more readily in its environment. I actually don't mulch my garden because I set my plants close together. By the time it is hot enough to mulch, the leaves shade the soil keeping it moist, cool, and practically weed-free.

Sidedressing

Sidedressing is the term for adding fertilizer to plants halfway through the growing season. Cabbages take a lot of nutrients from the soil so it is important to feed them again. The best time to sidedress cabbages is just as the heads are forming. Well-dried cow or horse manure, compost, or commercial fertilizer will provide the feast.

Using a spade, dig a circular trench 2 inches wide and 2 inches deep about 4 to 5 inches out from the stem of each cabbage. Add about a half-inch of fertilizer to the ring and cover it with the loosened soil. Be careful not to burn the leaves of the plant by getting manure or fertilizer on them. Water the plants well after sidedressing. Should the cabbages get too much of a good thing they might begin to split. Cabbages grow from the inside out. Over-fertilizing

To "cabbage onto some-thing" is to grab, snatch or steal something. To "cabbage someone into doing some-thing" means to trick or coerce the person.

causes the inside leaves to grow faster than the outer ones, and the head bursts open. If that is the case, take each head and twist it about a quarter turn. That will break off some of the secondary roots and slow its growth.

Cabbage's Natural Enemies

There are a number of garden pests that can ruin cabbage plants. Hand picking bugs, worms and slugs before they multiply to uncontrollable proportions is the most effective and simplest way to eliminate them. No products or materials are necessary. It does require daily monitoring to maintain healthy cabbages and limit vege-table loss. Try growing spearmint, pennyroyal, tomatoes, or garlic nearby, perhaps bordering the cabbage patch. A mulch of the same around plants will also help to ward off harmful insects.

Cabbage is one of the heartiest plants in the garden, so you will probably never see most of the cabbage-eating pests. The most common cabbage enemies are listed here with non-toxic ways to control their proliferation.

Cabbage Aphids, also called plant lice, suck juice from the leaves of cabbages causing them to curl and grow in a deformed way. The leaves are characterized by a sticky substance. Aphids are greenish blue when immature and black with wings as adults. Leaves infected with aphids should be removed immediately and discarded far from the other cabbages. Avoid overhead sprinkling of cabbages if aphids appear. Water by soaking instead, if possible.

Several harmless preparations can rid cabbages of aphids if used early. Washing the leaves with plain old soapy water can destroy existing aphids and their larvae. Aphids do not tolerate garlic, and leaves can be sprayed with a mild garlic solution to deter their development. Use

4 to 5 cloves per quart of water, blend, strain, and spray on aphids. Do not apply in the heat of the day to avoid burning the leaves. Both these

✤✤✤✤✤✤✤✤✤✤✤✤✤✤✤

A good way to clean pewter is to rub it with a cabbage leaf.

✤✤✤✤✤✤✤✤✤✤✤✤✤✤✤

treatments may require repeated applications and will work best if action is taken immediately upon spotting aphids.

Fighting fire with fire, use an alternative yet effective spray by making juice from dead aphids. This is a good one to apply should the insects get too numerous, however unsavory the task. Gather the leaves with large quantities of aphids and scrape the insects into a blender. Add water, blend and leave the solution several days to decompose and putrify. Strain and spray on plants to repel existing aphids. After trying this one summer, our garden aphids were eliminated and stayed away the following year as well.

Aphids attach themselves to the underside of plants out of direct sunlight. If you put aluminum foil on the ground around the cabbage stalks it will reflect light to the underside of the leaves, confusing the aphids. The insects will not as readily congregate on the cabbage leaves.

Helpful insects such as ladybugs, praying mantises and lacewing flies can be found or bought and set about among aphids. The house sparrow is also quite fond of eating aphids and can be encouraged to frequent your garden by the addition of a bird feeder or bird bath. Trees contribute greatly to a healthy, bug-free garden because trees attract birds which eat harmful insects.

Clay, in a diluted form, can be sprayed onto aphids to suffocate them. Tobacco dust can be purchased from garden supply centers and is an effective way to kill aphids. Fill a thin sock or cloth with a handful of tobacco dust and sprinkle it on the infestation of aphids.

Slugs and Snails can be a problem in humid climates during especially wet times. Traps can be laid to collect the

++*+*+*+*+*+*+*+*+*+*
*30 compounds make up the
composition of the wax
coating that forms on cabbages, protecting the heads.*
++*+*+*+*+*+*+*+*+*+*

slugs and snails by removing a few cabbage leaves to lie on the ground near the other plants overnight. In the morning the creatures will be on the loose leaves which can then be collected and the slugs and snails destroyed.

A dish of beer or honey and yeast in water near the cabbage plants will also attract slugs and snails which crawl in and drown. Wood ashes or lime on top of the soil around cabbage plants will act as a barrier to slugs and snails.

Salt conservatively sprinkled onto cabbages will be absorbed by the slugs and snails and will dissolve them. Rye flour sprinkled on cabbages overnight will form a glue with the evening and morning dew, coating the pests. As the dew evaporates the paste will harden and suffocate the slugs and snails. Once the slugs and snails bore into the cabbages, however, it is difficult to eradicate them with this method.

Worms. Several non-toxic methods exist for controlling all worms that attack cabbages, should you desire to avoid the use of chemical pesticides. These methods do not kill bees, earthworms and helpful insects such as the ladybug or praying mantis. These are some of nature's creatures which help sustain healthy soil and plants through aeration, fertilization, pollination and natural pest control.

Bacillus thuringiensis (B.t.) is a biological insecticide that is safe to use on all plants. It can be found under the brand names *Dipel* or *Thuricide*. B.t. contains a bacterium which forms a crystal that poisons the larvae of moths as they eat the treated plants. B.t. kills cabbage worms, cutworms, webworms, and cabbage loopers, as well as tomato hornworms. Earthworms are of a different category altogether and are not harmed by using *Bacillus thuringiensis*. B.t. is not harmful to humans or pets.

Pyrethrum is a powder made from a type of chrysanthemum containing a substance that is toxic to many insects, the imported cabbage worm and aphid included. It is not harmful to humans or animals and can be applied directly to foliage. Pyrethrum attacts the nervous system of the insects and renders them unconscious. They can then be collected and destroyed.

White Hellebore is a member of the lily family which is toxic to cabbage worms and slugs. A powder is made from the roots, or rhizomes, of the plant. When exposed to light the insecticide loses some of its toxicity and therefore has little residual effect.

Ways to Pick and Store Cabbage

Choosing the freshest cabbage in the grocery store or market is not difficult. Look at the cut stem to see how fresh the core looks. The core should not be split. check for a firm, compact head. Leaves should not be moldy or yellowish, and should be free of bug holes or other signs of pest damage. Red cabbages have a natural grey powdery appearance on the outer leaves which should not be

Market in Merida, Mexico. Photo by John Schoenwalter.

confused with spray residue. Never buy a cabbage that is already cut, as the vitamin C content will be greatly reduced.

Cabbage can be kept for several months in the refrigerator if covered in plastic wrap so it won't dry out. The secret to storing it for so long is to never cut into the head, unless it can all be used at once. Cabbage provides its own freshness seal with overlapping layers. When a few leaves are needed, peel off the outer leaves which will appear dry or wilted and discard them. Then take as many fresh leaves as you need. Wrap the head again in plastic and keep it in the refrigerator.

If you try growing your own cabbages, the ideal way to store them is to stagger the plants so as to have continual harvests. That way, they can be kept in the refrigerator and used one at a time. If that is not possible, due to a large crop or simultaneous maturity of the cabbages, the following tips will help you to store your plants throughout the winter months.

1. Check to determine if the cabbage is ready to harvest by pressing firmly on the head with the thumb. If it feels spongy it is not yet ready. If the head is firm and compact it may be harvested.

2. Select a dry day. Pull cabbages up with the roots in late afternoon when the plants are not wet. Do not wash cabbages or remove their outer leaves. Wet leaves promote rotting.

3. Ideal storage conditions are at 32 degrees F. with 90%—95% humidity. Cabbages will wilt if too dry. A root cellar will usually work fine.

4. Place each head in a paper sack and tie the open end closed with a string. Hang each by the string in a root cellar. The cabbages should store this way for 3 to 4 months.

Chapter V

THE CULINARY CABBAGE

Cabbageheads: wormy purple, silver-glaze,
A dressing of mule ears, mothy pelts, but green-hearted,
Their veins white as porkfat.
　　　Sylvia Plath, "Who," Crossing the Water

Say "cabbage" to anyone and usually cole slaw comes to mind. But that's often the only cabbage dish that people can think of. Many tend to see cabbage as a boring vegetable for lack of imaginative recipes to vary the fare. Red cabbage can add a complementary dash of color to salad greens, while savoy, with its rumpled leaves, varies the texture. Cabbage is not only versatile in its use, but is visually pleasing. On the crosscut, cabbage resembles a lace doily whose pattern can dress up many a vegetable dish.

For maximum health benefits, raw is the best way to eat cabbage. When exposed to heat, cabbage loses much of its high vitamin C content as well as the vitamin U (anti-pepsin for fighting ulcers), as both are water-soluble. Minerals are generally not affected by heat.

There are many savory cooked cabbage dishes, and the cabbage is still a nutritious food. Cooked cabbage does, however, impart a definite sulphuric odor and can cause intestinal gas, two more reasons for eating cabbage raw.

"... But I Can't Stand The Smell!"

All the members of the cabbage family contain compounds that form hydrogen sulfide when cooked, leaving that unmistakable odor of rotten eggs. If you're a corned beef and cabbage fan or adore cabbage rolls but hate to smell up the kitchen, here are a few ways that may reduce that rotten egg odor when cooking cabbage. One rule of thumb applies: less cooking time means less odor.

—Place a bowl of open vinegar next to the pot.

—Steam cabbage quickly over water which is already boiling. Drain the cabbage immediately and discard the water.

—Add a couple of slices of stale bread to the cooking water to absorb the odor.

—A rib of celery in the pot will reduce the smell of sulphur.

—Drop a whole walnut in with the cabbage as it cooks.

—Two or three savory leaves added to the cooking water help eliminate unpleasant odors and impart an agreeable flavor to cabbage.

What to Cook With Cabbage

Many other foods and herbs complement the taste of cabbage and can be added to ordinary recipes to alter the flavor. If you are the type of cook who enjoys experimenting to come up with your own tasty combinations, you can create imaginative cabbage dishes with some of the following:

Allspice brings out the sweetness of cabbage.

Blueberries—add fresh or frozen to a sweet cabbage salad.

Caraway seeds impart a strong flavor. Use them sparingly in salads or soups. In hot cabbage dishes, add seeds the last half hour to avoid bitterness from overcooking.

Dill adds a complementary taste to cabbage and is especially good in things pickled. Use it in cabbage salad recipes which call for vinegar.

Mint is good to add to a cream and lemon sauce for a refreshing cole slaw.

Pineapple enhances cabbage's natural sweetness and has a complementary taste.

Piñon nuts, with their sharp pine flavor, make an interesting partner with cabbage in salads or cabbage rolls.

Poppy seeds liven up all cabbage dishes, especially slaws.

Sage, used sparingly, is good for stuffed cabbage roll recipes which call for meat.

Sorrel gives cabbage recipes a tart flavor.

Sunflower seeds not only add a complementary flavor but a crunchy texture as well.

If you lack the time or desire to experiment and create your own recipes, the following ones have been tried and rated outstanding. I have included mostly recipes calling for raw cabbage, for obvious health reasons. However, several of the vegetable dishes require little cooking, such as stir-frying and steaming, and so are almost as nutritious. The cabbage roll recipes were just too good to pass up, even though cooked extensively.

Cabbage leaf veins.

Appetizers
❧❧❧

Cabbage Pinwheels

This recipe is quite simple to make, and the results are attractive spirals of dark and light green.

> 1 head green or savoy cabbage
> 1/2 lb. fresh spinach, Swiss chard or watercress
> 1/2 cup slivered almonds
> 1/4 cup sesame seeds
> soy or tamari sauce

Steam spinach, chard, or watercress for about 1 minute, then drain. Cool under cold running water and set aside to drain again. Steam cabbage leaves until pliable but not limp, about 2 to 3 minutes. Place cabbage so that leaves overlap one another on a flat cookie sheet, making a rectangle. Layer spinach on top of cabbage, covering completely. Sprinkle with almonds and sesame seeds. Roll the whole thing tightly from one end, and tie with string. Refrigerate at least a half hour. Cut into 1-inch slices and secure each with a toothpick. An hour before serving, sprinkle with soy sauce or with tamari, diluted with water.

An attractive bowl to use for an hors d'oeuvre tray is a cabbage rose made from a whole cabbage. Steam the head upside-down for a few minutes until the outer leaves can be easily pulled back, resembling a rose. Core the insides out and fill with dip.

Peanut Butter & Cabbage Snack

A nutritious and easy snack to fix for children or adults is to spread peanut butter on cabbage leaves and roll them up. The taste of the cabbage and peanut butter together is delicious and there is no need for sugary jellies or honey to moisten the snack. The cabbage leaves provide plenty of water to help make the peanut butter go down.

Soups
♣♣♣

Cabbage soup is traditionally prescribed in many European countries to remedy a hangover. Cabbage makes a hearty, hot soup for winter or a chilled borscht for summer. Serve soup as a main course with some crusty French rolls or a tossed salad for an easy-to-fix dinner.

Cabbage & Tomato Soup

The following recipe is simple to make, inexpensive, and, as an extra bonus, is low in calories. Serves 8.

> 1 medium size head of cabbage
> 1 large can of tomato juice (46 oz.)
> 46 oz. water
> 3 bouillon cubes
> juice of 1 fresh lemon
> salt & pepper to taste
> fresh basil, parsley, scallions, onions, celery,
>   tomatoes, peppers, carrots, etc. (optional)

Wash, drain, and shred cabbage. Place juice in a large non-aluminum saucepan with an equal amount of water. Add the cabbage and slowly bring to a boil. Cover and simmer for 10 minutes. Add the bouillon, lemon juice, salt, and pepper plus any other spices and vegetables you wish. Cover and cook slowly for another 5 to 15 minutes, depending on the degree of doneness desired for the other ingredients.

Should you have a tremendous hangover, this recipe easily makes about 8 to 10 servings. If less soup is desired, use a smaller can of juice and adjust the other ingredients proportionately. The soup tastes better the second day. For best results, reheat it very slowly. Cabbage and tomato soup freezes well.

♣ ♣ ♣

Constant reheating of any cabbage dish is not advisable. A 16th century author commented:

> . . . now this crambe (cabbage) was in olde tyme much used in feastes and bankettes, but if it were twyse sod it was so lothed and abhorred that the Grekes made a proverb on it. For as often as they wolde signifi a thyng agayne and agayne repeted, not without tedyousness a grevaunce, they sayde forthwith in theyr langage: Crambe twyse served is death.

That may be a bit overstated. To my knowledge, there are not fatalities on record caused by eating leftover cabbage. Most cabbage dishes are actually better the second day after the flavors have had a chance to blend. If reheated more than once, however, cabbage does develop a strong odor and slightly bitter flavor. The best approach is to warm it slowly.

Salads

✤✤✤

Sweet & Sour Cole Slaw

Here's a tasty recipe from France. Although this salad calls for whiskey, it also includes an alcohol antidote: cabbage. Not only will you not get intoxicated, but you'll enjoy the complementary taste of the spirits, raisins, pineapple and cabbage.

    vinegar
    1 head cabbage
    1 cup raisins
    1/2 cup whiskey
    1/2 cup fresh cream (or yogurt)
    juice of 1 lemon or 3 tbsp. vinegar
    4 or 5 drops tabasco sauce
    1/2 teaspoon salt
    1 can pineapple chunks, drained
    1/2 cup pecans (optional)

Three or four hours before serving, peel off cabbage leaves, cut out the thick veins and soak for about 20 minutes in a bowl of vinegar water. Wrap them in a towel to dry. Spread another dry towel beside working surface. Take 2 or 3 leaves and roll them tightly lengthwise like a cigar. Cut in fine slices and place them on the towel, continue until all leaves are sliced. Roll the towel tightly to absorb all the moisture and set aside.

Put raisins in a small bowl and cover with whiskey. In a larger salad bowl mix cream, lemon juice, tabasco, and salt. Add the sliced cabbage, stir to coat, and refrigerate until ready to serve. Add whiskey-soaked raisins, pineapple, and pecans just before serving.

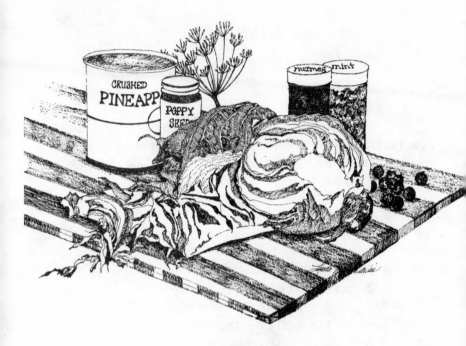

Cabbage and Cucumber Salad

Here is another recipe which capitalizes on the great taste com-
bination of cabbage and pineapple. Serves 6.

> 1 lb. green or white cabbage
> 1 fresh cucumber, peeled and sliced
> 1 can pineapple chunks or pieces of fresh
>   pineapple
> 2 tbsp. pineapple juice
> 1/2 cup sour cream
> 1/2 cup plain yogurt
> 1 tbsp. dill weed

Wash, core, and coarsely shred cabbage. Add cucumber slices and mix with juice, sour cream, yogurt, and dill.
Refrigerate at least one hour. Add pineapple just before
serving.

Apple, Orange, and Curry Slaw
Serves 6 to 8.

1 head shredded savoy cabbage
2 large tart green apples
1/4 cup orange juice
2 tbsp. lemon juice
3/4 cup vanilla yogurt
1/4 to 1/2 tsp. curry
dash salt
16 oz. can Mandarin oranges

Wash and prepare cabbage for coleslaw. Quarter and core but do not peel apples. Slice the apples thinly and add to the shredded cabbage. Mix all other ingredients except oranges and add sauce to the slaw. Toss and refrigerate. Add the drained Mandarin oranges before serving.

Cabbage Salad with Piñon Nuts
Serves 8.

1 small head of green cabbage
1 green pepper, sliced
2 tart green apples, sliced
1 cup shelled piñon nuts
juice of 1 lemon
1/4 cup cream
1/4 cup mayonnaise
salt to taste

Cut cabbage in half and soak for one hour in salted ice water. This will keep it crisp and make it easier to shred. Drain and shred the cabbage. Add the green pepper and apples. Mix the lemon juice, cream, mayonnaise and salt, pour over the salad, and refrigerate slightly. Just before serving add the piñon nuts.

Cabbage and Kidney Bean Salad
Serves 6 to 8.

1 small head red cabbage
1 small head green cabbage
1 medium red onion
1 can of kidney beans
1/4 cup red wine vinegar
1/4 cup virgin olive oil
juice of 1 lemon
salt and pepper to taste

Wash and shred cabbage. Chop onion and add to cabbage. Drain beans and mix with salad. Combine the last four ingredients and toss with cabbage, onion, and kidney beans. Refrigerate at least one hour.

Lite Cabbage Salad
This salad is low in calories, only about 80 per serving. Serves 6.

1 lb. green cabbage
1/2 lb. red cabbage
1 cup blueberries
3 chopped scallions
1 tbsp. chopped fresh
   parsley

Dressing:
1/4 cup dry white wine
1/4 cup virgin olive oil
juice of one lemon
salt and pepper to taste

Shred cabbage and mix with green onions and parsley. Refrigerate at least one hour. Mix ingredients for dressing and pour over cabbage one half hour before serving. Stir in blueberries just before serving.

Indonesian Cabbage Salad
Serves 6.

1 medium head broccoli, cut into florets
1 head sliced Chinese cabbage
1 red pepper, cut into strips
1 cup fresh bean sprouts
1/2 cup peanut halves

Sauce:
1/4 cup creamy peanut butter
1/4 cup boiling water
3 tablespoons soy sauce
1/4 cup chopped scallions
ground pepper

Steam broccoli 3 to 4 minutes or microwave until tender but still crisp. Cool and mix with cabbage, pepper, and sprouts. Combine peanut butter, water, and soy sauce. Stir until blended. Add scallions and pepper. Toss with salad, garnish with peanuts, and serve immediately.

❖❖❖❖❖❖❖❖❖❖❖❖❖❖❖❖❖❖❖❖❖❖❖❖❖❖❖❖❖❖❖❖❖❖

Chinese cabbage, "pai ts'ai," is the most common food in the Chinese diet. Cabbage, rice, soybeans, and mustard compose the basic diet of Chinese peasants.

❖❖❖❖❖❖❖❖❖❖❖❖❖❖❖❖❖❖❖❖❖❖❖❖❖❖❖❖❖❖❖❖❖❖

Vegetable Dishes

Colorful Cabbage Stir Fry
Serves 6 to 8.

2 cups thinly sliced green cabbage
2 cups thinly sliced Chinese cabbage
1 carrot, cut into julienne strips
1 each green and red bell peppers, julienne
1 yellow summer squash, julienne
2 tbsp. peanut oil

Sauce:
1/4 tsp. cinnamon
1/4 tsp. nutmeg
1 tsp. cornstarch
1 tbsp. fresh lemon juice
1 tbsp. soy or tamari sauce
2 cloves minced fresh garlic
1/2 tsp. minced ginger root

Mix all ingredients for the sauce and set aside. Prepare vegetables and toss together in a large bowl. Heat wok and when hot add peanut oil. Swish oil around in wok (away from open flame) to coat all sides. Add vegetables all at once and stir fry until they begin to wilt, about 2 minutes. Add sauce and cook another minute or until all vegetables are coated with sauce. Serve immediately.

To retain the color of red cabbage during cooking, add 1 tablespoon of white vinegar or lemon juice to 2 cups of cooking water.

Cabbage with Sour Cream Sauce

If you need a quick vegetable idea for dinner, this recipe is delicious and can be prepared in about 5 minutes. Serves 8.

1 head cabbage
1 tbsp. dill weed
2 tbsp. butter
1 cup sour cream
1 tbsp. vinegar
salt and pepper to taste

Cut cabbage into eights, wash, and remove core. Steam quickly in salted water until tender, about 4 or 5 minutes. Drain well and keep hot. Meanwhile, cook dill weed in butter for 1 minute. Add the sour cream, vinegar, salt and pepper. Stir until blended and hot. Pour over cabbage wedges and serve immediately.

Quartered red cabbage.

Sauerkraut

Sauerkraut is nutritionally as good as raw cabbage. In fact, because it is more compact, cup for cup it has more vitamins and minerals than cabbage. Even though it has the texture of cooked cabbage, there is no heat involved in the fermenting process, so water-soluble vitamins are not lost. It is higher in salt, which is sprinkled on the cabbage to break down the cells and soften the leaves. If your intake of sodium must be restricted, try rinsing the sauerkraut before using it in recipes.

Kim Chi

Kim Chi (also spelled Kim Chee) is an east Asian version of German-style sauerkraut. The coolies who built the Great Wall of China were fed Kim Chi and rice, and survived under heavy duress thanks to the wholesome balance of those two foods. Kim Chi has all the benefits of sauerkraut plus the added healthful properties of garlic, ginger, and cayenne, high in vitamin C.

    1 large head Chinese cabbage
    2 1/2 Tbsp. salt
    3 large cloves garlic, chopped
    1 tsp. grated ginger root
    1 to 2 Tbsp. cayenne pepper

Cut unwashed cabbage into pieces about 1 inch long. Sprinkle with 2 tbsp. salt and set aside for about 20 minutes until water drops form on the cabbage. Wash cabbage several times in cold water to remove salt. Layer cabbage, garlic, salt, ginger, and cayenne in a large glass jar and fill with water. Cover and let stand at room temperature 5 to 6 days. Refrigerate. This is good to eat after 2 or 3 days.

Plain Ol' Sauerkraut

cabbage
pickling salt
water
a glass or ceramic container

Most recipes call for a large 5-gallon crock, but sauerkraut can certainly be made in something smaller. Shred the cabbage rather finely and pack it in the container. Mix a 2% solution of brine, or 4 tsp. pickling salt per quart, and pour it over the cabbage. Put a plate over the top of the crock and let it ferment. When no more bubbles come up (about 4 to 7 weeks) it is time to can it. If you don't want to can the end product, I would suggest making enough to fill a one-gallon glass jar and eating it fresh. It is tasty after a week, so you can sample the sauerkraut throughout the fermenting process to see at what degree of doneness you prefer it. Sealed, the uncanned sauerkraut will keep in the refrigerator several weeks.

Football Fan Fare

This recipe is just the thing for serving during the playoffs or the Superbowl. It can be put together during the halftime break and be ready to eat in the 4th quarter.

sauerkraut
sliced ham
1 bottle beer

sliced Swiss cheese
    or sharp cheddar cheese
mustard

Roll sauerkraut in ham slices and arrange in a deep baking dish. Place cheese slices on top. Pour the beer over all and bake for 20 minutes at 350 degrees F. Garnish with mustard. Serve with rye bread and plenty of beer.

Cabbage Rolls
♣♣♣

Nearly every country of the world where cabbage grows has a prized cabbage roll recipe: in India, bhare bandh gobhi, in Russia, golubtsi, in Greece, dolmadas. The stuffings vary according to the traditional foods and spices of each locale, but the cabbage leaf wrappers do not change. Here are two international winners.

Krautburgers

This is a variation of the true cabbage roll. Instead of the stuffing being wrapped in cabbage leaves, German krautburgers are cabbage filling baked in bread dough. Makes 24.

1 pkg. 24 frozen dinner rolls
1 tbsp. olive oil
1 lb. lean ground beef
1 large chopped onion
1 head shredded green or white cabbage
1 tsp. horseradish
5 drops tabasco sauce
1/4 cup tomato sauce
salt & pepper to taste

Thaw rolls and let raise while preparing filling. Sauté onion in olive oil until transparent, add ground beef, horseradish, tabasco, tomato sauce, and salt and pepper. Cook slowly, covered, about 10 minutes, then add shredded cabbage. Cook briefly then turn off heat. Drain on paper towels if too oily.

Roll out bread rolls to 1/8 inch thickness, forming a 5

inch square. Place 2 to 3 tbsp. cabbage mixture on each square, fold corners and pinch edges to seal seams. Place the sealed side down on a greased cookie sheet. Brush tops and sides with oil. Cover and let raise 15 minutes.

Bake in a pre-heated oven at 400 degrees F. for 20 minutes or until golden. Serve hot.

Greek Cabbage Rolls Avgolemono

This is a delicious vegetarian cabbage roll recipe that is best made a day ahead. Serves 6.

2 medium heads savoy cabbage
3 tbsp. butter
1 onion
1 cup water
1 cup white rice
1/2 cup raisins
1/2 cup piñon nuts
1/4 cup chopped fresh parsley
1/4 cup chopped fresh dill
salt and pepper to taste

Avgolemono sauce:
3 eggs
juice of 1 large lemon
2 tbsp. butter
1 1/2 cups reserved cabbage liquid

Wash and steam cabbage leaves until pliable but not limp, then drain and set aside. Sauté chopped onion in butter until transparent. Add the water and rice and bring to a boil. Cover and simmer until rice has absorbed the water, about 15 to 20 minutes. Remove from heat and add the next four ingredients, then season with salt and pepper. Separate two eggs and add the whites to the filling. Use the two yolks in the egg lemon sauce.

Place a heaping tablespoon of filling in each cabbage leaf, fold ends to the middle and roll up snugly. Place them in a casserole pan with the seam side down. Dot with butter, add water to cover and simmer for one hour, covered. Using a slotted spoon, transfer rolls to a platter, keeping them warm. Strain the liquid, saving 1 1/2 cups.

Beat the 2 egg yolks and the remaining egg well. While continuing to beat eggs, add the lemon juice gradually, then the hot liquid very slowly until all has been added. Cook the sauce over hot but not boiling water, stirring constantly, until it coats a wooden spoon. Pour over the cabbage rolls and serve immediately. Garnish with fresh parsley or dill sprigs.

Red cabbage, cross-cut.

Desserts

Chocolate Sauerkraut Cake

Chocolate and sauerkraut sound like an unlikely pairing of tastes and textures in, of all things, a cake. The kraut actually adds moisture to the cake's natural dryness and helps prevent it from spoiling—if it should last that long. The trick to a successful sauerkraut cake is to purée the sauerkraut so as not to have tell-tale cabbage fibers in the cake. No one will ever guess the secret ingredient.

> 1 cup sauerkraut
> 2 cups flour
> 1 tsp. baking soda
> 1 tsp. baking powder
> 1 1/4 cups sugar
> 2/3 cup shortening or butter
> 3 eggs
> 1 tsp. vanilla
> 2/3 cup unsweetened cocoa
> 1 cup water

Rinse sauerkraut under cool water, drain. Rinse and drain again. Put in blender or food processor with a small amount of the cup of water if necessary, and blend until finely chopped, then set aside. Sift together flour, soda, and baking powder, and set aside. Cream sugar and shortening. Add eggs one at a time, beating well after each addition. Mix in vanilla and cocoa. Add flour mixture alternately with water. Fold in sauerkraut. Bake in a 9 x 13" greased and floured cake pan at 325 degrees F. for 30 to 35 minutes. Cool before icing.

Icing

1 cup sour cream
1 12 oz. pkg. cream cheese
1/4 cup honey
1/4 tsp. vanilla

Soften cream cheese and mix with sour cream, honey, and vanilla. Spread on cooled cake. For a marbled icing effect dribble melted chocolate on icing and then streak swirls with a knife.

Cabbagehead Chocolate Cake

Any plain chocolate cake recipe or mix can be turned into a work of art by brushing melted chocolate over cabbage leaves as a mold, and then arranging the leaves (after peeling off the cabbage) around the cake baked in circular bowls. The result is a beautiful dark chocolate cabbagehead that will astound your guests.

1 box chocolate cake mix to make 2 layers
2 – 1 1/2 quart round stainless steel mixing bowls
1 pound semi-sweet chocolate
6 to 8 whole cabbage leaves (not savoy)
2 cups chocolate mousse or chocolate icing

Preheat oven to 325° F. Mix batter for chocolate cake as directed. Grease and flour the round mixing bowls and divide batter evenly between the two bowls. Place both on a cookie sheet and bake 30 to 35 minutes. Cool the layers completely before removing from the bowls, about 2 to 3 hours.

Meanwhile, melt the chocolate over water and brush a thin layer over the backs of the cabbage leaves. Prop them over cups or bowls to retain their natural curve, if necessary. Refrigerate for about 10 minutes. Peel off the cabbage and refrigerate chocolate leaves again until ready to use.

Prepare chocolate mousse or icing. When cake layers are thoroughly cooled, remove them delicately from the bowls. Spread a layer of the mousse between the cake layers, saving at least 2/3 to cover the cake. Spread the remaining mousse over the entire cake ball and cover with chocolate cabbage leaves to form a round head. Refrigerate until ready to serve.

A beautiful head of green cabbage.

Chapter VI

AILMENTS & CABBAGE REMEDIES

*To be rare, to come from a far-away country, to bear
an exotic name and to have an inflated value, are
factors that put a price on a medicine and which are
entirely lacking in the cabbage leaf.* —Dr. A. Blanc

Ways To Prepare Cabbage For Medicinal Use

Juice. Cabbage is one of the best tonics for health and
is inexpensive health insurance. It is rich in vitamins and
minerals that nourish the body and help digestion and
elimination. Cabbage juice, if made freshly and drunk
immediately, is pleasant-tasting and can be sweetened by
the addition of a spoonful of honey. Other variations that
are delicious include:

1.
50% green cabbage
25% celery
25% carrot

2.
50% green cabbage
20% orange
20% papaya
10% strawberry

3.
75% green or red cabbage
25% fresh pineapple

4.
75% green cabbage
25% melon

Please note, however, that cabbage juice is only good
when fresh. The sulphur and other minerals in the cabbage
begin to oxidize within about 10 to 15 minutes, creating an

offensive smell. Equally, the pulp must be disposed of to avoid leaving a disagreeable odor. The vitamin C in cabbage will also start to deteriorate immediately due to exposure to light and air, so it is best to consume the juice just as soon as it's made. There are commercially prepared juices available, however, the taste of these tends to be unpleasant and, more often than not, they are juices extracted by vapor with a loss of nutrients in the process.

Prepare fresh cabbage juice with the use of a juicer, food processor, or blender (a little water must be added to facilitate the liquefying process in the blender). Chop the cabbage into wedges if using a juicer or food processor, into small pieces for a blender. After obtaining pulp, strain it through a cheesecloth or a strainer.

Salad. There are many delicious recipes for salads using raw cabbage that can add nutritious variety to a daily menu. Use cabbage effectively in any recipe calling for lettuce (i.e., sandwich greens, tossed salad). It is far more healthful. For ideas see Chapter V.

Sauerkraut. Sauerkraut and its oriental equivalent, Kim Chi, are two types of pickled cabbage that retain all the essential vitamins and minerals found in raw cabbage. This is so because the cabbage is not heated, which destroys water-soluble vitamins, but rather "cooked" without heat in a brine solution. Kim Chi has the added benefits of garlic and cayenne, both high in vitamin C. Both sauerkraut and Kim Chi can be eaten raw and the juice of either substituted for raw cabbage juice, except when sodium intake is restricted. See Chapter V for specific recipes.

Poultice. Obtain a cabbage poultice by taking enough fresh cabbage leaves to apply 3 or 4 layers to the affected area. In winter, warm them first to avoid chilling the body. This can be done in several ways: 1.) by dipping the leaves in hot water for 30 seconds; 2.) by placing them on the lid of a pot of hot liquid until limp; or 3.) by leaving several cabbage leaves out of the refrigerator for 15 minutes.

Next, crush the leaves to bring the juice to the surface. This requires taking a rolling pin or bottle and rolling firmly over the leaves. Remove the large center vein first in order to crush the leaves uniformly. Place them with the top, crushed side against the skin and secure them with an elastic bandage or a tightly fitting garment.

Maurice Mességué, a well-known French herbalist who has helped popularize the tradition of folk remedies, softens and heats cabbage leaves by ironing them "until they are as soft as velvet." He adds that, "Even people in severe pain smile at this trick."

Crushed cabbage leaf, prepared for poultice.

Warning

Please use common sense in following any of the remedies listed below. The use of cabbage to treat any illness is not suggested as an alternative to proper medical care, but rather as a preliminary step or a dietary supplement. In many cases, modern medicine has come up with more efficient treatment of ailments. Excessive consumption of cabbage may possibly be harmful; especially for someone suffering from goiter or hypoglycemia. Consult your health care professional before changing your diet.

List of Ailments and Remedies

✤ **Abscess**—*(a skin inflammation accompanied by some sort of infection.)* See also Carbuncles. Cabbage has an absorbative effect on pus and will reduce the swelling of any inflammation. An old Anglo-Saxon remedy calls for using cabbage leaves as a poultice for "black blains," pustules, or blisters. **Uses:** Apply several layers of crushed cabbage leaves to the abscess. When excessive heat from the infection is felt, reapply fresh leaves.

✤ **Acne**—*(inflammation of the oil glands and hair follicles of the skin, characterized by pimples, whiteheads, and blackheads.)* A German folk remedy calls for the application of crushed inner white cabbage leaves on the face and affected areas for acne, rash, German measles, and herpes. A cabbage facial mask can rejuvenate the skin by absorbing impurities and sterilizing the skin tissues. Cabbage promotes blood circulation; the tingling sensation of the skin is the effect of increased circulation. **Uses:** Have ready the extracted pulp from three medium-sized cabbage leaves. Wash face thoroughly. Steam face for 10–12 minutes, making a tent with a towel over a pot of boiling water. Thyme, sage, basil, mint and lavender are all good for the skin. These herbs added to the water can be beneficial as well as pleasant smelling.

Once pores are opened, dry face quickly and pat the

cabbage pulp onto the skin avoiding the area around the eyes. For extra dry skin a teaspoon of olive oil can be added to pulp; for oily skin mix in a teaspoon of plain yogurt. When mask is in place, lie down with feet raised for 15 to 20 minutes. Sponge off pulp with warm water or warm milk. Rinse face with warm water to which a little apple cider vinegar has been added. This acts as a natural astringent to close pores.

For individuals with sensitive or broken skin, cabbage may be irritating. They are cautioned to first try the pulp on a small area of skin to determine if there is a reaction. If so, rinse immediately with milk.

♣ **Alcoholism.** (See also Hangover and Liver in this list, and Alcoholism, Hangover, and Cirrhosis of the Liver in Chapter II). Vitamin B6 is commonly given to alcoholics, and cabbage is high in this vitamin. French folk remedies suggest eating raw or steamed cabbage or drinking cabbage juice to offset the effects of alcohol. They also recommend cabbage in the same manner for cirrhosis of the liver. **Uses:** Prepare fresh cabbage juice. If you know you will be drinking heavily, down a glass of it beforehand. After too much alcohol, drink some juice to help avoid a hangover the next day. A fresh salad of cabbage can be eaten prior to drinking alcohol. Even cooked cabbage is beneficial to counteract the effects of alcohol in the body, and many cultures have a favorite cabbage soup recipe for this reason (see Chapter V).

♣ **Anemia.** *(A deficiency of oxygen-carrying material in the blood, caused by the lack of any one of several nutrients in the body: iron, protein, folic acid, vitamins B-6 and B-12.)* Cabbage is an excellent food source containing iron and vitamin B-6, a lack of which causes types of anemia. One cup of the vegetable shredded contains 6% RDA of iron. Though they tend to be bitter, the outer leaves of the green types contain the highest yield. Unfortunately, when you buy cabbage in the store these leaves are usually removed. If you grow your own cabbage, be sure to keep these iron-rich outer leaves. Their taste will sweeten after a frost or two.

♣ **Animal Bites.** See Bites.

♣ **Appetite Loss.** The ancient Romans, renowned for their food orgies, found they could eat more at any one sitting if they began and ended their meals with cabbage.

♣ **Arteritis.** *(Inflammatory disease of the arteries.)* **Uses:** Dr. Valjean, author of *The Treatment of Illness by Vegetables, Fruits and Grains,* advises applying 3 or 4 layers of crushed cabbage leaves to the legs overnight to help restore circulation and ease pain. He notes that cabbage alone will not cure arteritis, but that it is of indisputable aid.

♣ **Arthritis.** *(The painful condition of inflammed joints of the body.)* See also Inflammations. To aid the sinews and joints, Cato recommended drinking the water cabbage had been boiled in. Elderly people in France often put crushed cabbage on their hip and knee joints when afflicted with arthritis or rheumatism. These are held in place by long underwear during the cold winter months. **Uses:** Apply several layers of warmed cabbage leaves over the painful joints and secure with an elastic bandage or a tightly-fitting garment. This is most practically done overnight.

♣ **Bites.** *(Animal, Insect, or Snake.)* Philistion prescribed cabbage bouillon mixed with barley meal to apply to snake bites. Epicharmus recommended cabbage for treating the bite of the shrew-mouse. In popular French herbology, Dr. Valjean advises the use of fresh cabbage for insect bites. **Uses:** As soon as possible after the bite, rub the area with a bruised cabbage leaf. Wrap the bite afterwards with several layers of crushed cabbage leaves. Bites of any type can be extremely serious, especially if poisonous; therefore, it is important to see a health care professional.

♣ **Bladder.** Cabbage is esteemed by the Chinese as a natural diuretic, having the property of helping urine flow through the bladder and system. **Uses:** Apply 3 layers of crushed cabbage leaves on the lower abdomen for urine retention, day and night if necessary. Drink 1 to 2 glasses a day of fresh cabbage juice.

❧ **Boils.** (*Painful, pus-filled swelling of tissue under the skin and subcutaneous tissue caused by bacterial infection.*) See Abscess and Carbuncles for cabbage remedies.

❧ **Bronchitis.** (*A chronic or acute inflammation of the mucous membrane of the bronchial tubes.*) See also Inflammations in this list, also Colds, Sore Throat and Bronchitis in Chapter II.

Cabbage has been used in France for centuries as an effective cure for the soreness and deep congestion of bronchitis. Though it requires repeated applications of cabbage leaves to the chest, the results can be quite remarkable. The cabbage leaves absorb toxins through the skin. When combined with fresh juice as a gargle, this plant remedy breaks up a cough and helps eliminate phlegm. **Uses:** Crush 3 or 4 fresh cabbage leaves and apply to the chest, throat or general area of discomfort. Secure and leave several hours or overnight. During the winter the leaves should be warmed slightly to prevent chilling the body. They should *not* be cooked or allowed to become limp, however. Gargle and drink a fresh glass of cabbage juice made from 3 to 4 medium-sized leaves every 4 hours or as pain of sore throat returns. The direct contact of the juice on the throat will usually burn slightly, but it seems the more it burns the better its effect.

❧ **Bruises.** Because cabbage contains vitamin K, which helps clot blood, it is a good food source to consume in order not to bruise easily. Cabbage is beneficial for promoting circulation to all parts of the skin and system; therefore, when applied topically, it helps clear up bruises. **Uses:** Apply several layers of crushed leaves to the bruised area, reapplying every 4 to 6 hours. Internally, consume raw cabbage in salad or fresh form at least 3 times a week to help strengthen the walls of the blood vessels.

♣ **Burns.** For minor sunburns, as well as other first and some second degree burns (for third degree see a physician), application of cabbage leaves will help relieve the pain and heal the scarred tissues. Apply cabbage as soon as possible after the burn occurs. **Uses:** Wrap 3 or 4 cool, crushed cabbage leaves over the burn and leave on 2 or 3 hours or overnight.

♣ **Bursitis.** *(An inflammation of a bursa, a fluid-containing sac or cavity that reduces friction between a tendon and bone.)* See Arthritis and Inflammations for uses.

♣ **Cancer.** *(The pathological condition characterized by the growth of malignant tumors which tend to invade healthy tissue and spread to new sites.)* See Cancer in Chapter II.

Studies show a positive relationship between eating cabbage and the prevention of cancer. No conclusive evidence exists to support cabbage as a cure for existing cancer. However, if you have cancer and your physician does not object to your eating cabbage, try the following applications. **Uses:** Eat one serving per day of raw cabbage, in salad or juice form. Apply a poultice of crushed cabbage leaves externally over the cancerous area. Change poultice every 3 to 4 hours.

♣ **Carbuncles.** *(A painful, infected swelling of the skin which can sometimes be fatal.)* Refer to Abscess for uses. Dioscorides advised applying cabbage and salt to carbuncles to cause them to burst.

♣ **Chilblains.** *(Inflammation, usually of hands, feet and ears, followed by itchy irritation caused by exposure to moist cold.)* See Inflammations.

♣ **Colds.** *(A viral infection of the mucous membranes of the respiratory passages.)* See Colds, Sore Throat, and Bronchitis in Chapter II. A German folk remedy advises drinking raw sauerkraut juice as a preventive measure to avoid getting a cold. **Uses.** Gargle and swallow fresh cabbage juice at the onset of a cold to act as a deterrent. For an existing condition gargle and swallow fresh cabbage juice every 3 to 4 hours. As a further precaution or in the case of severe or more developed symptoms, a poultice of 3 to 4 layers of crushed or ironed cabbage leaves can be applied to the throat and chest overnight. An elastic bandage or a tightly-fitting garment can be use to hold the leaves in place over-night.

♣ **Colitis.** *(Inflammation of the large intestine.)* See also Inflammations and Cancer. **Uses:** Externally, cover the abdomen with 3 or 4 layers of crushed cabbage leaves at night, and secure. Internally, drink 1 to 3 glasses of freshly-extracted cabbage juice between meals. A juice made of half cabbage and half carrots is also recommended. Should the treatment last over a month, several days repose should be taken.

♣ **Conjunctivitis.** *(Inflammation of the conjunctiva, the mucous membrane connecting the eyelid to the eyeball.)* See also Inflammations. **Uses:** According to the noted French herbalist, Maurice Mességué, drops of fresh cabbage juice in the eyes will help conjunctivitis. Prepare juice and add 2 drops to eyes every 3 to 4 hours. Apply an eye pack to closed eyes made of crushed fresh cabbage leaves, 3 to 4 layers thick. Leave in place 20 minutes. Continue applica-tions several days or until condition improves.

♣ **Constipation.** *(Infrequent, incomplete and difficult bowel movements, often accompanied by gas.)* See also Diarrhea, Dysentery, and Intestines in this list. Cabbage provides fiber for roughage which means that it helps carry foods through the digestive system, aiding in a normal elimination of the bowels. Raw cabbage eaten on a regular basis will help prevent bowel problems. **Uses:** For cases of constipation, 2 to 4 glasses of cooked cabbage broth or fresh cabbage juice should be drunk each day. Raw sauerkraut is also esteemed to be an effective laxative.

♣ **Corns.** *(A thickening of the skin, usually on a toe, resulting from pressure or friction.)* **Uses:** Apply strips of a crushed cabbage leaf externally over the corn to ease the

Savoy leaf.

pain. Better yet, use the cabbage as a dressing to hold a clove of crushed garlic over the corn. Secure and leave overnight. If done during the daytime, change every 4 hours.

♣ **Cough.** See also Bronchitis. Raw cabbage juice can be gargled and swallowed to soothe the irritated throat tissues. French herbalists recommend making a cough syrup of equal parts of red cabbage juice and honey. **Uses:** Warm freshly-extracted cabbage juice only enough to be able to dissolve honey in it. This syrup must be prepared fresh each time you use it. Dose: 2 large spoonfuls five times daily.

♣ **Cuts.** See also Wounds. It has been observed that workers in sauerkraut factories seldom have infections from cutting or bruising themselves when they handle fresh cabbage. Because of its broad leaf shape, cabbage makes a practical bandage for use in dressing cuts. Vitamin C, of which cabbage is a good source, is important to collagen production. Collagen acts as a connective agent for cells, hence aiding the regrowth of cuts without excessive scarring. **Uses:** Wash the cut area well and apply a dressing of crushed cabbage leaves which will help keep the cut sterile and promote healing of the tissues.

♣ **Cystitis.** *(Inflammation of the bladder.)* See Bladder and Inflammations for uses.

♣ **Deafness.** Cato prescribed drops of warm cabbage juice mixed with wine in the ears to cure deafness. German peasants also use a similar recipe for improving their hearing: equal parts wine and cabbage juice, dropped frequently in each ear. **Uses:** Make juice from fresh cabbage leaves and apply 2 drops in ears every 3 to 4 hours.

♣ **Diabetes.** *(A severe, often inherited metabolic disorder of the pancreas in which the body does not produce enough insulin to metabolize sugar from carbohydrates in the diet.)* Recent studies on dietary influences on diabetes indicate that fiber has a preventive effect on diabetes mellitus (infantile). Raw cabbage is recommended for its high fiber content. One study on medical botany (Lewis and Elvin-Lewis) lists cabbage and turnips as insulin substitutes. **Uses:** Add cabbage to the diet, in conjunction with the standard treatment for diabetes, if your doctor OK's it.

♣ **Diarrhea.** *(The excessive evacuation of watery feces which can cause a serious depletion of bodily fluids.)* See also Dysentery and Constipation. Although it may seem contradictory, raw cabbage is recommended in herbal texts for both constipation and diarrhea because it normalizes the intestines and prevents bowel problems. **Uses:** Wash 2 or 3 whole cabbage leaves and eat them raw, chewing thoroughly. Warmed cabbage leaves, rolled and crushed, should be applied two or three layers thick to the lower intestines and changed every 4 hours or left overnight. Once the diarrhea has stopped, drink 2 to 3 glasses a day of fresh cabbage juice to help replace lost fluids.

✤ **Dysentery.** *(An infection of the lower intestinal tract producing pain, fever, and severe diarrhea, often with blood and mucus.)* See also Diarrhea, Intestines and Constipation. A Chinese herbal advises ingesting raw cabbage for dysentery or bloody stools.

✤ **Ears.** See also Deafness. Contrary to popular belief, cabbage will not cure a cauliflower ear.

✤ **Eyes.** See Conjunctivitis. Ancient Greeks prepared an eye wash of fresh cabbage juice with a little honey to remedy swollen, runny eyes. Mattioli, a 17th century Italian physician, recommended cabbage for those with troubled eyesight. Dioscorides said that "Being eaten, it helps those who are dull-sighted."

✤ **Gangrene.** *(Death and decay of bodily tissue caused by loss of blood supply, injury, or disease.)* Also see Wounds in this list, and Varicose Veins and Gangrene in Chapter II. **Uses:** Since gangrene is a very serious condition requiring the attention of someone licensed in health care, cabbage poultices are recommended in the absence of or until obtaining professional assistance. Wrap 3 to 4 layers of crushed cabbage leaves over damaged area. Secure with an elastic bandage being careful not to constrict the flow of blood. Change every 2 to 3 hours.

✤ **Gastritis.** *(Inflammation of the stomach, especially the lining.)* See Inflammations and Ulcers also. Karen is a friend who became my guinea pig for treating gastritis with cabbage. When I met her, she had suffered for years from the debilitating pain of gastritis. I suggested she try cabbage juice and, although she insisted she'd tried everything over the years, she did juice some fresh cabbage and drank it. Within half an hour her gastric pains were gone. Karen now keeps a couple of heads of cabbage in her refrigerator at all times.

✤ **Gingivitis.** *(Inflammation of the gums, often with bleeding.)* See also Inflammations. Because of its high vitamin C content, cabbage is beneficial for maintaining gums in a healthy state. **Uses:** Prepare fresh cabbage juice. Hold the juice in the mouth and rinse the gums well with it before swallowing. The direct contact of cabbage juice on the gums will reduce swelling and promote healing of the cells.

♣ **Goiter.** *(A chronic enlargement of the thyroid gland.)* Goiter is caused by a lack of iodine in the diet and the thyroid gland's inability to produce adequate levels of hormones in the body. See also Inflammations. **Caution: Persons who have a lowered ability to assimilate iodine should be cautioned that eating excessive amounts of cabbage and raw nuts may interfere with iodine utilization in the production of the thyroid hormone, thereby compounding the iodine deficiency.** Check with a physician before changing your dietary regimen. One book recommends taking a kelp supplement to increase iodine if cabbage is eaten often. French herbalists advise drinkng fresh cabbage juice for goiter, as well as wrapping the neck with several layers of crushed cabbage leaves.

♣ **Gout.** *(A metabolic disorder that results in arthritis-like attacks of pain when crystals of improperly metabolized uric acid lodge in muscles and joints.)* Gout can be brought on by over-indulgence in food, alcohol, or by kidney disease, certain medicines, surgery, or infections. See also Inflammations. Dioscorides praised cabbage for treating gout, saying "with the meal of fenugreek and vinegar, it helps those who have gout in their feet and in their joints." Cato recommended a linament of cabbage, rue, and coriander for gout and diseases of the joints. **Uses:** Modern herbal medicine suggests a poultice of warm cabbage leaves on the swollen feet and hands.

♣ **Hangover.** See also Alcoholism and Liver in this list, and Alcoholism, Hangover, and Cirrhosis of the Liver in Chapter II. Nearly every European country has its favorite recipe for cabbage soup to remedy the effects of too much alcohol in the body (see Chapter V). **Uses:** Immediately after drinking too much alcohol and especially before going to bed, consume raw cabbage in any form: juice, salad, or 2 to 3 plain leaves.

✤ **Hair Loss.** Though he did not specify in what way to use cabbage, Dioscorides said that it would keep hair from falling out. The Chinese use the oil extracted from cabbage seeds (*Brassica chinensis*) which they rub on the scalp in an effort to promote hair growth. Philistion recommended mixing cabbage with a ball of alum in vinegar and rubbing it on the head to prevent hair from falling out.

✤ **Headache.** Cato advised eating cabbage for severe headaches. **Uses:** Apply 3 or 4 crushed cabbage leaves to the area where pain is most intense.

✤ **Hemorrhoids.** *(Swelling of a vein or veins in the anal region, often accompanied by bleeding.)* See also Inflammations. **Uses:** Apply one small crushed cabbage leaf, rolled and used as a suppository, to reduce swelling and pain. Reapply every 4 hours.

✤ **Herpes.** See Acne and Skin.

✤ **Hoarseness.** See Laryngitis.

✤ **Hypoglycemia.** *(Low blood sugar syndrome.)* Paavo Airola contends that certain foods, among them vegetables of the cabbage family, contain oxalic acid which can be harmful to hypoglycemics if eaten in large quantities raw. He recommends cooking it and then discarding the water.

✤ **Impotence.** See Prostate.

✤ **Indigestion.** *(The inability to digest food, often resulting in excess acid in the stomach.)* Indigestion can be caused by eating too fast, or by being tired, or under stress. See Indigestion and Ulcers, Chapter II. A common treatment in France for indigestion is to eat 2 or 3 spoonfuls of raw sauerkraut. **Uses:** Prepare fresh cabbage juice. Or blend a cabbage leaf in one cup of water. Drink the liquid one hour after eating, then again after two more hours.

✤ **Infections.** See also Cuts and Wounds. Cabbage leaves contain an antibiotic called rapine which is effective against certain fungi. Infections are serious enough to warrant seeking professional medical advice. In the interim or for minor infections, a cabbage poultice will promote increased circulation to an infected area, the blood containing the necessary white corpuscles to fight the infection. Cabbage is especially good at drawing pus out of infected areas. **Uses:** Remove the large center veins from 3 or 4 fresh cabbage leaves and bruise them. Apply the poultice of cabbage leaves to the infection once it is clean. Wrap securely with an elastic bandage. For serious infections, consult a physician immediately. Equally effective is to chop cabbage and carrot to obtain a fine pulp. Place on the infected area, cover with 1 or 2 crushed cabbage leaves, and secure with a bandage. Change the dressing every 2 hours. It is possible that as the cabbage absorbs the toxins from the skin, the infection will break and exude pus. Rinse with salt water and reapply a fresh dressing until the infection is cleared.

♣ **Inflammations.** (including arteritis, arthritis, chilblains, colitis, conjunctivitis, cystitis, gastritis, goiter, gout, hemorrhoids, laryngitis, lupus, neuritis, phlebitis, pleurisy, prostatitis, rheumatism, sinusitis, sprains, varicose veins; – *"itis" is a suffix indicating the inflammation of the area in question.*) According to Maurice Mességué, cabbage excels all other vegetables in drawing out the pain of any inflammation and in helping to reduce the swelling. I observed the rapid healing power of cabbage applied to a minor puncture wound and inflammation of a friend's leg. At the moment of the accident the skin immediately began to swell creating a bruise the size of a silver dollar on her shin. After putting four crushed cabbage leaves over her leg and wrapping it with an elastic bandage left on overnight, the next morning the spot that had been injured was neither bruised nor swollen. All that remained was a faint half-inch mark where the skin had been cut. **Uses:** Externally, apply a poultice of crushed leaves to the area.

Internally, drink 2 or 3 glasses of freshly extracted juice each day, before meals.

✤ **Insect Bites.** See Bites.

✤ **Insomnia.** *(Chronic inability to sleep.)* See also Nightmares. Cato the Elder recommended eating boiled and salted cabbage in large amounts to prevent insomnia. Since boiled cabbage is very gas producing, it is hard to imagine that this would be as effective a remedy as eating raw cabbage in some form. The gas pains might further inhibit restful sleep. For sleeplessness, French herbalists recommend going to bed in the evening with 3 layers of cabbage leaves on the nape of the neck and sometimes on the legs.

✤ **Intestines.** Cabbage contains beneficial quantities of calcium, iodine, potassium, chlorine, and sulphur which are minerals that cleanse the mucous membranes of the stomach and intestines. Regular consumption of raw cabbage is helpful for allowing a smooth passage of food through the intestines. Raw cabbage usually does not create gas, but in many individuals cooked cabbage is flatulent. Though the mineral content of cabbage is not altered by cooking, its vitamin C and U factors are destroyed by heat. It is always preferable to eat cabbage raw for maximum health benefits. Studies have shown that cancer of the colon and intestines are possibly prevented by including raw cabbage in the diet. (See Cancer.) Germans eat sauerkraut to disinfect the intestines. Its enzymatic action is beneficial upon foul, congested matter in the bowels. **Uses.** For intestinal infection, it is recommended to take a small glassful of fresh cabbage juice or sauerkraut juice each morning before eating. Otherwise, for healthy intestines, regular consumption of raw cabbage or raw sauerkraut is advised (see recipes in Chapter V).

♣ **Laryngitis.** *(Inflammation of the larynx, the upper part of the respiratory tract containing the vocal chords, resulting in* *a loss of voice.)* Dioscorides prescribed cabbages because "being chewed, and the juice swallowed down, they restore the loss of voice." In France, a known preventive measure taken among opera singers and actors to keep from losing their voices is to gargle and drink equal parts of cabbage juice and honey, or to drink unsalted cabbage bouillon to which an egg yoke has been added and slightly beaten. **Uses:** Laryngitis occurs when the larynx is inflamed, and cabbage is extremely effective in reducing tissue swelling. Make fresh cabbage juice, gargle, and swallow it. The longer the juice is held in contact with the throat, the better its effect. Equally, add honey to slightly warmed juice and drink as a soothing syrup for the voice.

✤ **Liver.** See Alcoholism and Hangovers in this list, also Alcoholism, Hangovers, and Cirrhosis of the Liver in Chapter II. A sourcebook from France advises applying a warm poultice of chopped cabbage leaves and watercress mixed with a beaten egg. Wrap the mixture in a cheesecloth and apply over the abdomen. For cirrhosis of the liver the ingestion of cabbage is recommended in any form: juice, raw or steamed vegetable, or sauerkraut.

✤ **Lupus.** See Inflammations.

✤ **Measles.** See Acne.

✤ **Menopause.** *(The natural discontinuance of a woman's menstrual cycle, often accompanied by physical and psychological trauma.)* One American doctor and author of medical booklets states that for the proper passage through menopause one needs ample amounts of potassium to maintain proper adrenal functioning. He recommends one serving daily of raw cabbage instead of lettuce as a salad green. One cup of shredded raw cabbage provides 10% RDA (recommended daily allowance) of potassium. Other nutritional source books state that a lack of calcium contributes to hot flashes and irritability in menopause. Absorption of calcium in the body is reduced when the production of estrogen decreases. Cabbage is recommended for supplying adequate amounts of calcium, which is especially found in the darker green outer leaves. One cup of chopped cabbage can provide 12% of the daily recommended allowance of calcium.

✤ **Menstrual Cramps.** Hippocrates stated that cabbage promotes menstrual discharge. **Uses:** Warm several cabbage leaves and crush them to bring the juice to the surface of the leaves. Apply as a poultice on the lower abdomen where cramps are felt.

✤ **Migraine.** See Headaches.

✤ **Motherhood.** Ancient Athenian physicians prescribed cabbage for nursing mothers so their babies would grow robust and strong, and throughout ancient Greece, cabbage was fed to women giving birth. Hippocrates claimed that cabbage increases the quantity of milk in nursing mothers. Cooked cabbage, which produces gas, should be avoided because the baby can also suffer from intestinal gas and may experience discomfort. Raw cabbage is best to eat. Newborn babies have a temporary deficiency of vitamin K. Most hospitals routinely give newborns doses of vitamin K to help them establish healthy blood coagulation. Cabbage is high in vitamin K.

✤ **Muscular Pains. Uses:** Take warm, crushed cabbage leaves, or iron leaves until smooth and moist on the lowest setting of the iron. Apply several layers over the muscle in pain and bandage. Change the dressing every 2 to 3 hours.

✤ **Neuritis.** *(Inflammation of a nerve, often resulting in pain, loss of reflexes and muscular atrophy.)* For pain or inflammation of the nerves, one German folk remedy suggests eating raw sauerkraut. A medicinal plant book from France recommends several layers of cool, crushed cabbage leaves along the nerve. These are left in place at least 4 hours or overnight. Repeated applications are suggested before improvement can be noticed. Another French remedy, however, suggests a compress of hot chopped cabbage leaves wrapped in a cheesecloth, placed over the painful nerve.

♣ **Nervousness.** The calcium and sulphur in cabbage allow it to help calm the nerves. It is especially beneficial for those who suffer from anxiety, depression, insomnia or who are chronically tired. **Uses:** 2 glasses of fresh cabbage juice a day are recommended for a general tonic for healthy functioning of the nerves. See page 90 for tasty variations on cabbage juice.

♣ **Nightmares.** See also Insomnia. For preventing unpleasant dreams and insomnia, Pliny the Elder extolled the virtue of cabbage when boiled and salted, and eaten by itself. However, boiled cabbage often produces gas which might cause very unrestful sleep. For that reason, raw cabbage would be preferable. Another prescription popular in France for dispelling nightmares is to drink cabbage water with sage added to it. **Uses:** Bruise a cabbage leaf by rolling over it with a rolling pin and put it and some crumpled sage in a liter of water. Leave it several hours. Strain, and drink 2 to 3 cupfuls a day.

♣ **Nosebleed.** An old remedy advises wrapping cabbage leaves over the nape of the neck.

♣ **Obesity.** Though cabbage itself will not directly cure obesity, it provides a very nutritious food source with a low caloric intake. One cup of raw shredded cabbage contains only 17 calories. The same amount made into coleslaw prepared with vinegar or lemon juice has a scant 25 calories; made with mayonnaise, 100. It is an extremely good food to include in any weight reduction program. Cabbage also provides roughage which helps carry food through the digestive tract and thereby eliminates stress on the bowels and intestines of individuals who are obese from overeating.

♣ **Pancreatitis.** *(Inflammation of the pancreas, which can lead to diabetes mellitus in severe cases.)* See also Diabetes. Consumption of cabbage is recommended to prevent such an inflammation.

Cabbage leaf veins.

✤ **Phlebitis.** *(Inflammation of the veins.)* See Inflammations. **Uses:** Apply a poultice of 3 or 4 layers of cabbage leaves to the entire chest area, changing the dressing every 3 or 4 hours or overnight. Drink 1 to 2 glasses of fresh cabbage juice a day.

✤ **Poisoning.** In ancient times Appolodorus claimed that cabbage seeds or fresh juice could remedy poisoning by fungi. A current book on medical botany (Lewis and Elvin-Lewis) states that the antibiotic *rapine,* which is extracted from cabbage, is useful for counteracting poisoning by fungi.

✤ **Prostatitis.** *(The swelling of the prostate, the male reproductive gland that surrounds the urethra near the bladder.)* Epicharmus stated that nothing is more beneficial for diseases of the testes and genitals than cabbage. Cabbage is good as a back-up treatment to be used in conjunction with other remedies for prostatitis (pumpkin seeds and fresh parsley are two additional reported dietary remedies). **Uses:** For pain and swelling of the prostate, apply a poultice of cabbage leaves one night on the perineum, one night on the lower abdomen. If necessary, apply day and night. Drink a glass of freshly prepared cabbage juice daily.

♣ **Rheumatism.** *(The condition of inflammation and discomfort of the joints, bones and muscles.)* See also Arthritis. One of the reasons cabbage may be helpful for rheumatism is because of its calcium content. In a book on plants and their uses *(Summary of Common Plants,* 1782), the author, Dr. Chonnel, recommends applying a salve prepared with one white cabbage head and some potter's clay. Cover the cabbage and clay in water and cook slowly in an earthern pot until the mixture is completely reduced to a pulp. This salve should be applied warm. **Uses:** Apply a poultice of hot cabbage leaves to the affected area. Bandage and leave overnight.

♣ **Scurvy.** *(The deficiency of Vitamin C, characterized by anemia, weakness, bleeding from mucous membranes, and spongy gums.)* See Scurvy in Chapter II. Cabbage has so much vitamin C that by weight it ranks with orange juice. **Uses:** Eat one serving of raw cabbage or sauerkraut daily to treat existing scurvy, two or three servings a week for prevention.

♣ **Sinusitis.** *(Inflammation of the sinuses.)* See also Inflammations. **Uses:** Dr. Valjean advises applying 3 layers of crushed cabbage leaves on the sinuses as well as inhaling one half teaspoon of fresh cabbage juice in each nostril, mornings and evenings.

♣ **Skin.** (eczema, skin rash, German measles, ringworm, impetigo.) Applying crushed cabbage leaves to the skin, even for a half hour, will revitalize the surface tissues, promote circulation, cleanse pores and absorb impurities.

Apply only to clean skin, bandage well enough for the leaves to stay in place. Leaving on overnight is highly recommended. For sensitive skin a small patch should first be tested for a reaction. A German remedy calls for using only the inner white leaves on the skin, after removing the thick center vein. Equally, fresh cabbage juice can be sponged onto the skin. **Uses:** A cabbage facial and tonic once a week are recommended as a treatment for health and beauty. Individuals with sensitive skin, however, are advised to first try a small amount of cabbage pulp on their skin to determine if there is a reaction. See Acne for instructions for cabbage mask.

♣ **Snake Bites.** See Bites.

♣ **Sore Throat.** See Bronchitis in this list and also Colds, Sore Throat, and Bronchitis in Chapter II. **Uses:** For an existing sore throat prepare fresh cabbage juice every 3 to 4 hours to gargle and swallow. (For cabbage juice recipes see page 90.) For additional benefit apply a poultice of ironed or crushed cabbage leaves to the throat overnight.

♣ **Sprains.** *(An injury, usually to the ankle or wrist, resulting in the twisting of a ligament or a muscle without dislocating the bones.)* Cato recommended beating up cabbage leaves twice a day and applying them to sprains. **Uses:** A warm poultice of cabbage leaves bandaged snugly around the sprain facilitates the elimination of accumulated liquid within the sprain and helps reduce swelling. It should be renewed morning and night.

♣ **Tonsillitis.** *(Inflammation of the tonsils, lymphoid tissue in the aperture between the mouth and the pharynx.)* See also Sore Throat and Bronchitis. Gargling fresh cabbage juice will cleanse the throat and heal by the direct contact of the juice on the throat. A poultice applied to the neck and chest overnight will aid in reducing swelling and drawing out toxins to relieve the pain. **Uses:** Prepare fresh cabbage juice using a blender, juicer or food processor. Strain the pulp, and gargle and swallow the juice. Repeat every 3 to 4 hours or as pain reoccurs. Apply a poultice on the throat area using enough warm cabbage leaves to provide at least 3 layers. Wrap with an elastic bandage or a snug garment. Leave on overnight if possible, or change every 3 to 4 hours.

♣ **Ulcers.** *[An inflammatory lesion on an internal mucous membrane surface of the body, most generally of the stomach (duodenal and peptic).]* See Indigestion and Ulcers in Chapter II. A Russian remedy for ulcers is to drink 4 to 5 glasses of fresh cabbage juice daily, for one week. **Uses:** Cabbage juice should be taken with or after meals for ulcers, not on an empty stomach. 75% cabbage and 25% celery is also an effective variation that does not alter the vitamin U content of the juice. Make fresh cabbage juice. Dose: 1 quart juice per day.

♣ **Varicose Veins.** *(The enlargement of veins due to blood vessels being blocked and the surface veins carrying more blood.)* See Varicose Veins and Gangrene in Chapter II. Eating raw cabbage daily will have a beneficial effect on varicose veins by providing fiber in the intestinal tract to relieve pressure of gas-producing material that collects there. Roughage is essential for proper movement of food through the digestive tract. When it moves slowly, unaided by roughage to carry it through, this material exerts pressure on the pelvic veins that can cause the leg veins to swell. **Uses:** Apply a poultice of leaves to the affected area, using 3 or 4 crushed leaves. Bandage loosely and leave on overnight. Cabbage promotes rapid circulation which may occasionally bring on a rather immediate and painful sensation. If this is the case, apply crushed leaves for only one to two hours, then wait 6 to 12 hours before reapplying.

♣ **Warts. Uses:** Apply fresh cabbage juice to help eliminate warts.

♣ **Worms.** Though the days of widespread intestinal worms are passed, cabbage has historically been used to

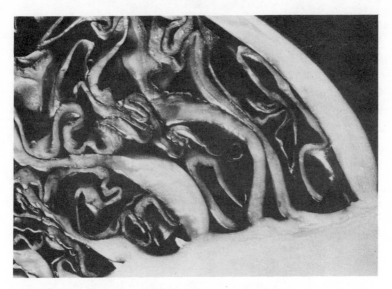

Red cabbage, cut detail.

effectively expel worms. A long-standing German tradition to rid the body of worms is to drink wine to which cabbage seeds have been added and steeped. One French folk remedy calls for drinking a glass of fresh cabbage juice for the first 3 days of the waxing moon. This can be accompanied by an application of crushed cabbage leaves on the abdomen overnight. Repeat the treatment every month at the same time for 3 to 4 months.

♣ **Wounds.** See also Cuts. Ancient Roman soldiers and also French troops in World War II used cabbage leaves, in the absence of proper wound dressing, to bandage their wounds. Maurice Mességué has said the following about cabbage used as a wound dressing. "Many a distinguished doctor has not hesitated to bind a cabbage leaf over a particularly nasty wound, despite the risk of being called a quack. The results have always been remarkable." Cabbage makes an ideal first aid bandage because it is antiseptic and promotes the production of collagen, with its high vitamin C content, to help tissues heal without scarring.

Uses: Serious wounds should be attended to by a physician. Cabbage is recommended to use only as a temporary dressing until professional medical attention can be obtained. Make sure the wound is absolutely clean to avoid an infection. Cut out the thick center vein of each cabbage leaf. For extremely sensitive wounds remove other large veins. The leaves can be softened and made more pliable by first dipping them in boiling water. They can also be left to macerate in olive oil for one hour, which will make them adhere better, and they will have the added healthful properties of olive oil. Apply 3 to 4 layers of the leaves over the wound and secure with an elastic bandage. Change the dressing every 2 to 3 hours.

Savoy leaf, reverse side.

BIBLIOGRAPHY

Airola, Paavo. 1977. *Hypoglycemia—A Better Approach.* Health
Plus Publishers, Phoenix, AZ.

Bianchini, Francesco and Francesco Corbetta. 1975. *The
Complete Book of Fruits and Vegetables,* Cro Publishers,
New York. Trans. by Italia & Alberto Mancinelli, introd.
by Maurice Mességué.

Boland, Maureen & Bridget. 1977. *Old Wives' Lore for
Gardeners.* The Bodley Head, London.

Buchman, Dian Dincin. 1973. *The Complete Herbal Guide to
Natural Health & Beauty.* Doubleday & Co., Inc., New
York.

_____. 1979. *Herbal Medicine: The Natural Way to Get
Well and Stay Well.* Gramercy Publishing Co., New York.
Illus. by Lauren Jarrett.

"The Cabbage: Eighty-Seven Remedies. Recipes Mentioned
by Cato and Opinions of the Greeks Relative Thereto,"
The Natural History of Pliny, Vol. IV. 1856. Trans. by
John Bostock and H.T. Riley. Henry G. Bohn, London.

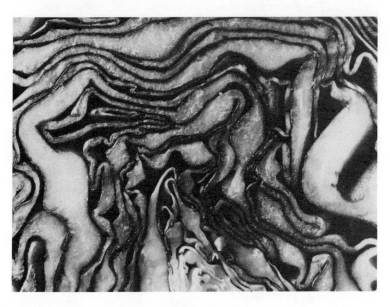

Red cabbage, cross-cut.

"Cabbage," *Fruit and Vegetable Facts and Pointers.* Jan. 1969. United Fresh Fruit & Vegetable Association, Washington D.C.

Camp, Wendell H., Victor R. Boswell and John R. Magness. 1957. *The World In Your Garden.* National Geographic Society, Washington D.C.

"Captain James Cook (1728-1779)", Aug. 25,1969. *Journal of the American Medical Association.* Vol. 209, No. 8.

Cheney, Garnett. Sept., 1950. "Anti-Peptic Ulcer Dietary Factor (Vitamin U) in the Treatment of Peptic Ulcer," *Journal of the American Dietetic Association,* Vol. 26.

_____. Jan., 1949. "Rapid Healing of Peptic Ulcers in Patients Receiving Fresh Cabbage Juice," *California Medicine,* Vol. 70.

Chinese Medicinal Herbs. 1973. Comp. by Li Shih-chen, trans. by F. Porter Smith and G.A. Stuart. Georgetown Press, San Francisco.

Chup, Charles and Arden F. Sherf. 1960. *Vegetable Diseases and Their Control.* John Wiley & Sons, New York.

Clark, Linda A., M.A. 1973. *Know Your Nutrition.* Keats Publishing, Inc., New Canaan, Connecticut.

Cook, James. 1776. "The Method Taken for Preserving the Health of the Crew of His Majesty's Ship the *Resolution* during her Late Voyage Round the World," *Philos Trans.,* Vol. 66.

Diet, Nutrition and Cancer. 1982. National Academy Press, Washington, D.C.

Diet, Nutrition & Cancer Prevention: A Guide to Food Choices. Nov. 1984. U.S. Department of Health and Human Services, NIH Publication No. 85-2711.

Donsbach, Dr. Kurt W. 1977. *Menopause.* The International Institute of Natural Health Sciences, Inc., Huntington Beach, California.

Dufty, William F. 1975. *Sugar Blues.* Chilton Book Co., Radnor, Pennsylvania.

Encyclopedia of Herbs and Herbalism, The. 1979. ed. Malcolm Stuart. Crescent Books, New York.

Ferguson, Marilyn. 1980. *The Aquarian Conspiracy: Personal and Social Transformation in the 1980's.* J.P. Tarcher, Inc., Los Angeles.

Folkard, R. 1892. *Plant Lore, Legends, and Lyrics.* London.

Food in Chinese Culture: Anthropological and Historical Perspectives. 1979. K.C. Chang, ed. Yale University Press, New Haven.

García Alcover, Blás. 1942. *Vitaminas y medicina herbaria.* Editorial Cultura, Santiago, Chile.

García Barriga, Hernando. 1974. "Flora medicinal de Colombia," *Botánica Médica.* Vol. I. Universidad Nacional, Bogotá.

Garland, Sarah. 1979. *The Complete Book of Herbs & Spices.* The Viking Press, New York.

Gerard's Herbal: The Essence thereof distilled by Marcus Woodward, 1636. Ed. by Th. Johnson. 1964. Spring Books, London.

Greene, Bert. 1984. *Greene on Greens.* Workman Publishing, New York.

Grieve, M. 1974. *A Modern Herbal.* 2 Vols. Hafner Press, New York.

Griggs (Van der Zee), Barbara. 1981. *Green Pharmacy: A History of Herbal Medicine.* Viking Press, New York.

Gunther, Robert T. 1959. *The Greek Herbal of Dioscorides,* (Trans. by John Goodyear 1655.) Hafner Publishing Co., New York. Illus. by a Bizantine (512 A.D.).

Harris, Ben Charles. 1970. *Kitchen Medicines.* Pocket Books, New York.

Haughton, Claire Shaver. 1978. *Green Immigrants: The Plants that Transformed America.* H. B. Jovanovich, New York.

Hausman, Patricia. 1983. *Foods That Fight Cancer.* Rawson Associates, New York.

Hehn, Victor. 1885. *The Wanderings of Plants and Animals from their First Home.* Swan Sonnenschein and Co., London.

Hunter, Beatrice Trum. 1971. *Gardening Without Poisons,* 2nd ed. Houghton Mifflin Co., Boston.

Inglis, Brian. 1965. *The Case for Unorthodox Medicine.* G.P. Putnam, New York.

Kourennoff, Paul M., and George St. George. 1971. *Russian Folk Medicine.* Pyramid Publications, New York.

Krutch, Joseph Wood. 1976. *Herbal.* David R. Godine, Boston.

Lawson, John Cuthbert. 1964. *Modern Greek Folklore.* University Books, New York.

Lehane, Brendan. 1977. *The Power of Plants.* McGraw-Hill Book Co., New York.

Leighton, Ann. 1970. *Early American Gardens: For Meate or Medicine.* Houghton Mifflin Co., Boston.

Lewis, Walter H. and Memory P.F. Elvin-Lewis. 1977. *Medical Botany: Plants Affecting Man's Health.* John Wiley & Sons, New York.

Long, Patricia J. and Barbara Shannon. 1983. *Nutrition: An Inquiry into the Issues.* Prentice-Hall, Inc. Englewood Cliffs, New Jersey.

Lovelock, Yann. 1972. *The Vegetable Book: An Unnatural History.* St. Martin's Press, New York.

Lucas, Richard. 1966. *Nature's Medicine.* Universal-Award House Inc., New York.

Lust, John. 1974. *The Herb Book.* Benedict Lust Publications, New York.

Luther Burbank: His Methods and Discoveries and their Practical Application, 1914. John Whitson, Robert John and Henry Smith Williams, eds. Vol. VII. Luther Burbank Press, New York.

Makanowitzky, Barbara (Norman). 1972. *Tales of the Table: A History of Western Cuisine.* Prentice-Hall, Inc. Englewood Cliffs, New Jersey.

Masefield, G.B., M. Wallis, S.G. Harrison and B.E. Nicholson. 1969. *The Oxford Book of Food Plants.* Oxford University Press, London.

Mazza, Irma Goodrich. 1973. *Herbs for the Kitchen.* Arco Publishing Co., New York.

Savoy leaf.

McDonald, Lucile. 1971. *Garden Sass: The Story of Vegetables.* Thomas Nelson, Inc., New York.

McLean, Teresa. 1980. *Medieval English Gardens.* Viking Press, New York.

Medicines from the Earth: A Guide to Healing Plants, 1978. William A.R. Thomson, M.D., ed. McGraw-Hill Book Co., New York.

Mességué, Maurice. 1979. *Health Secrets of Plants & Herbs.* Trans. by William Collins Sons & Co., Ltd. William Morrow and Co., Inc., New York.

_____. 1974. *Maurice Mességué's Way to Natural Health and Beauty.* Trans. by Clara Winston. Macmillan, New York.

_____. 1973. *Of Men and Plants: Autobiography of the World's Most Famous Plant Healer.* Macmillan, New York.

Morrison, Gordon. 1973. "The Cabbage Clan," *Horticulture,* May.

Newcomb, Duane. 1982. *Rx For Your Vegetable Garden.* J.P. Tarcher, Inc., Los Angeles.

Nutrition Almanac. 1975. Nutrition Search, Inc. John D. Kirschmann, Dir., McGraw-Hill Book Co., New York.

The Organic Way to Plant Protection. 1966. J.I. Rodale and staff, Glenn F. Johns, ed. Rodale Press, Inc., Emmaus, Penn.

Paananen, Eloise. 1984. *Of Cabbages and the King.* Betterway Publications, Inc., White Hall, Virginia.

Pearson, Durk and Sandy Shaw. 1982. *Life Extension: A Practical Scientific Approach.* Warner Books, Inc., New York.

Pelstring, Linda and Jo Ann Hauck. 1974. *Food to Improve Your Health: A Complete Guide to Over 300 Foods for 101 Common Ailments.* Walker & Co., New York.

Philbrick, Helen and Richard Gregg. 1966. *Companion Plants and How to Use Them.* The Devin-Adair Co., Old Greenwich, Connecticut.

Philbrick, Helen and John Philbrick. 1974. *The Bug Book: Harmless Insect Controls.* Garden Way Publishing, Charlotte, Vermont.

Pizer, Hank. 1982. *Guide to the New Medicine: What Works, What Doesn't.* William Morrow & Co., New York.

Quinn, Vernon. 1942. *Vegetables in the Garden and Their Legends.* J.B. Lippincott Co., New York.

Raymond, Dick and Jan. 1980. *The "Gardens For All" Book of Cauliflower, Broccoli & Cabbage.* Gardens for All, Burlington, Vermont.

Reilly, Dr. Harold J. and Ruth Hagy Brod. 1975. *The Edgar Cayce Handbook for Health Through Drugless Therapy.* Jove/HBJ Books, New York.

Riley, James Whitcomb. 1937. "Bub's Fairy Tale," *The Complete Poetical Works of James Whitcomb Riley,* The Bobbs-Merrill Co., Indianapolis. Preface by Donald Culross Peattie.

Riotte, Louise. 1975. *Planetary Planting: A Guide to Organic Gardening by the Signs of the Zodiac.* Simon & Schuster, New York.

Riotte, Louise. 1975. *Secrets of Companion Planting*. Garden Way Publishing, Charlotte, Vermont.

Rousseau, Jean-Jacques. 1979. *Pure Curiosity: Botanical Letters and Notes Towards a Dictionary of Botanical Terms*. Trans. by Kate Ottevanger. Paddington Press, Ltd., New York. Illus. by Pierre Joseph Redoute.

Shive, William Ph.D. "Glutamine as a General Metabolic Agent Protecting Against Alcohol Poisoning." (symposium paper—no date.)

_____, et. al. Nov. 1957. "Glutamine in Treatment of Peptic Ulcer," *Texas State Journal of Medicine*, Vol. 53.

Skinner, Charles M. 1939. *Myths and Legends of Flowers, Trees, Fruits, and Plants*. J.B. Lippincott Co., Philadelphia.

Sokolov, Raymond. May/June 1977. "Cabbage Fit for Kings," *The Saturday Evening Post*.

Sturtevant's Edible Plants of the World. 1972 (1919). ed. V.P. Hedrick. Dover Publications, Inc., New York.

Tannahill, Reay. 1973. *Food in History*. Stein & Day, New York.

Thistleton-Dyer, T.F. 1889. *Folklore of Plants*. London.

Thompkins, Peter and Christopher Bird. Nov. 1972. "Love Among the Cabbages: Sense and Sensibility in the Realm of Plants," *Harper's Magazine*.

_____. 1973. *The Secret Life of Plants*. Harper and Row, New York.

Valnet, Dr. Jean. 1975. *Traitement des maladies par les légumes, les fruits, et les céréales*, 5th ed. Librairie Maloine, Paris.

Winter, Evelyne. 1972. *Mexico's Ancient and Native Remedies: A Handbook of Testimonials and Historic References for Modern Use*. Editorial Fournier, Mexico, D.F.

INDEX

♣ A ♣

Ailments treated with cabbage, 93-114
abscess, **93,** 96, 97
acne, 10, 44, **93,** 103, 106, 111
alcoholism, **30,** 44, **94,** 102, 106
allergies, 43, 44
anemia, **94,** 110
animal bites, 23, **95**
appetite loss, **95**
arteritis, **95,** 104
arthritis, 44, **95,** 97, 102, 104, 110
asthma, 43
bites, 22, 23, 44, **95,** 105, 111
bladder, 43, **95,** 110, 109
boils, **96**
bronchitis, 14, 15, **32,** 43, 83, **96,** 97, 99, 111
bruises, 10, 15, 46, **96**
burns, **97**
bursitis, **97**
cancer, 12, 24, **27-30, 97,** 98, 105
   colon, 29
   esophagus, 30
   gastric, 29
   indoles, and, 29, 120
   intestinal, 30, 105
   rectal, 29
carbuncles, 93, 96, **97**
chilblains, **97,** 104
cirrhosis of the liver, **30,** 94, 102, **106**
colds, **32-34,** 43, 96, **97,** 111
colitis, **98,** 104
conjunctivitis, **98,** 101, 104
constipation, **98,** 100, 101
corns, **98**

cough, 43, 96, **99**
cuts, **99,** 103, 113
cystitis, **100,** 104
deafness, **100,** 101
diabetes, **100,** 108
diarrhea, 43, 44, 98, **100,** 101
dysentery, 22, 98, 100, **101**
ears, 97, 100, **101**
eyesight, 22, **101**
fevers, 23
gangrene, 10, **36-38, 101,** 112
gastritis, 43, **101,** 104
genitals, 23, **110**
gingivitis, **101**
goiter, 43, *93,* 102, 104
gout, 23, **102,** 104
hair loss, **103**
hangover, **30-32,** 73, 74, 94, **102**
headache, **103**
heartburn in pregnancy, 34
hemorrhoids, 15, 16, 44, **103,** 104
herpes, 93, **103**
hiccups, 23
hoarseness, **103**
hypoglycemia, 9, 93, **103,** 115
impotence, **103**
indigestion, 16, 34, **103,** 112
infections, 12, **44,** 99, 102, **103**
inflammations, 12, 95-98, **104,** 109, 110
insect bites, 44, **95, 105**
insomnia, **105,** 108
intestines, 29, 30, 43, 98, 100, 101, **105,** 108
laryngitis, 103-**105,** 106
liver, 30-32, 44, 48, 94, 102, 106

lupus, 104, **106**
measles, 93, **106**, 110
menopause, **106**
menstrual cramps, **107**
migraine, **107**
motherhood, **107**
muscular pains, **107**
nervousness, 46, **108**
neuritis, 104, **107**
nightmares, 105, **108**
nosebleed, **108**
obesity, **108**
pancreatitis, **108**
phlebitis, 104, **109**
poisoning, 22, **109**
prostatitis, 104, **109**, 110
rheumatism, 95, 104, **110**
scurvy, **38-39**, 44, 110
sinusitis, 104, **110**
skin, 43, **44**, 93, 94, **110-111**
snake bites, 22, 23, 44, **95**, **111**
sore throat, 14, 15, **32-34**, 96,
    97, **111**
sprains, 104, **111**
testes, 23, **110**
tonsillitis, **111**
ulcers, 10, 12, 16, 23, **34-36**,,
    44, **45**, 69, 101, 103, **112**
varicose veins, 16, **36-38**, 44,
    101, 104, **112**
warts, **112**
worms, **112-113**
wounds, 44, 46, 48, 99, 101,
    103, **113-114**
Airola, Paavo, 103
Akhenaton, 13
Alaska, Matanuska Valley, 57
Allspice, 70
American Institute for Cancer
    Research, 30
Aphids—see Gardening, pests

Apothecaries, 24
Apple, Orange, and Curry Slaw,
    77
Aristotle, 31

♣ **B** ♣
Bacillus thuringiensis (B.t.), 66
Backster, Cleve, 58
Beans, pole, 62
Beethoven, 34
Blanc, Dr. A., 90
Blondel, Dr., 59
Blueberries, 70, 78, 79
Bonesetting, 25
Brassica, 49, 50, 52, 103
    mustard, 49, 50, 62, 83
    rutabagas, 49
    turnips, 49, 100
Brassica chinensis, 50, 103
Brassica oleracea acephala, 49
Brassica oleracea botrytis, 49
Brassica oleracea capitata, 10, 23,
    49, 52
Brassica oleracea caulo-rapa, 49
Brassica oleracea gemmifera, 49
Brassica pekinensis, 50
Broccoli, 18, 19, 28, 29, 49, 79
Brussels sprouts, 18, 19, 28, 29,
    49
Burbank, Luther, 19
Buttermilk, 62

♣ **C** ♣
Cabbage
    appetizers, 72
    Chinese, 49, 50, 52, 53, 79, 80,
        83
    cooking odor, ways to reduce,
        70
    desserts, 87-89
    frost affecting, 50, 53-55, 95
    gas, and, 69, 107

green, 28, 53, 72, 76-78, 80, 84, 90, 94, 107
growing—see Gardening
juice, 14, 15, 34, 35, **90-92,** 94, 96-103, 105-113; frozen, 36
loopers—see Gardening, pests
love, and, 57-60
medicinal use of, preparation for **90-92**
nobility, and 12-13
per capita consumption, 41
poultice, 14, 18, **91,** 93, 97, 98, 102, 104, 106, 107, 109, 110-112
recipes, 12, 41, 61, **69-89,** 91, 94
red, 18, 32, 45, 48, **52,** 67, 69, 78, 90, 99
rolls, 53, 70, 71, **84-86**
salads, 70, 71, **75-79, 91**
Savoy, 44, 46-48, 52, **53,** 69, 72, 77, 85, 88
soups, 70, **73**
storage of, 67-68
two-headed, 51-52
varieties, 51, **52-54**
vegetable dishes, 71, **80-81**
warning, 93
wild, 18, 21-23, 49
worms—see Gardening, pests
Cabbage, & Tomato Soup, 73
Cabbage and Cucumber Salad, 76
Cabbage and Kidney Bean Salad, 78
Cabbage Pinwheels, 72
Cabbage Salad with Piñon Nuts, 77
Cabbage with Sour Cream Sauce, 81
Cabbagehead Chocolate Cake, 88
Captain Cook, 38

Caraway seeds, 70
Carroll, Lewis, *Through the Looking Glass,* 10
Cartier, Jacques, 22
Cato the Elder, 23, 24, 28, 30, 95, 100, 102, 103, 105, 111
    De re rustica, 23
Cauliflower, 12, 18, 19, 28-30, 49, 101
Celery, 61, 70, 73, 90, 112
Celts, 21, 22
Cerebral palsy, 45
Chamomile, 25, 60
Charlemagne, 52
Cheney, Dr. G., 35, 36
China, 12, 83, Chinese, 22, 25, 26, 95, 101, 113
Chiropractic, 25
Chocolate Sauerkraut Cake, 87
Chonnel, Dr., *Summary of Common Plants,* 110
Chrysippus, 22
Collagen, 41, 48, 99, 113
Collards, 19, 29, 49
Colorful Cabbage Stir Fry, 80
Cutworms—see Gardening, pests

♣ D ♣

DNA—see Nucleic acids
Dam, H., 45
Danish, 45, Denmark, 32
Dieuches, 23
Dill, 61, 70, 76, 80, 85, 86
Dionysius, 31
Dioscorides, 22, 38, 97, 101-103, 106, *De materia medica,* 22
Dipel—see *Bacillus thuringiensis* (B.t.)
Dishwater, 62

♣ E ♣

Egypt, 22; Egyptians, 13, 15

England, 21, English, 12, 21, 50
Epicharmus, 23, 95, 109

♣ F ♣
Fairies, 17
Ferguson, Marilyn, *The Aquarian Conspiracy*, 42
Findhorn—see Scotland
Football Fan Fare, 83
Foot reflexology, 34
France, 10, 12, 14, 21, 22, 25, 26, 32, 37, 38, 75, 95, 96, 106-108
French, 12, 26, 37, 73, 92, 94, 95, 98, 99, 102, 105, 107, 113

♣ G ♣
Gandhi, Mohandas, 14
Gardening, 12, 50, 117, 120
    companion plants, 60-62
    fertilizer, 50, **51**, 56, 59, **63**
    hardening off, 54
    late crop, 51
    manure, 50, 63
    mid-season crop, 51, 53
    mulching, 62, 63
    pests, 52, 57, 60, 62, 63, **64-67**
        aphids, 60, 62, 64, 65
        cabbage loopers, 66
        cabbage worms, 66
        cutworms, 66
        non-toxic ways to control, 64-67
        slugs, 64-67
        snails, 65, 66
        webworms, 66
    root depth, 50
    seedlings, 50, 51, **54-56**
    sidedressings, 63
    spacing of plants, 55-60
    sprouting seeds indoors, 54
    transplanting, 54, 55
Geraniums, 60

German, 18, 32, 49, 83, 84, 93, 97, 100, 107, 110, 111, 113
Glutamine, 36
Grapevines, 31, 62
Greece, 22, 84, 107; Greek(s) 13, 22, 24, 31
Greek Cabbage Rolls Avgolemono, 85

♣ H ♣
Hemp (*Cannabis sativa*), 62
Herbalists, 24, 99, 102, 105
Herbals, 26
Herbology, 20, 25, 95
Hippocrates, 20, 22, 107
Homeopathy, 14, 25
Hyssop, 61

♣ I ♣
Indoles—see Cancer
Indonesian Cabbage Salad, 79
Ionia, 13
Irish, 32
Italy, 22
IU (International units)—see Vitamins, retinol equivalents

♣ J ♣
Jupiter, 13

♣ K ♣
Kale, 19, 29, 45, 49
Kim Chi, 82, 91
Kohlrabi, 19, 49
Krautburgers, 84

♣ L ♣
Lincoln, Abraham, 123
Lite Cabbage Salad, 78
Lycurgus, 31

♣ M ♣

Marigolds, 60
Marijuana—see Hemp
Mattioli, 32, 101
Mességué, Maurice, 92, 98, 104, 113
Mexican, 33
Minerals, 19, 41, 42, 45, 48, 50, 51, 57, 69, 82, 90, 91, 105
    calcium, 41, 42, 45, 46, 105-108, 110
    iron, 41, 42, 48, 94, 95, 107
        hemoglobin, 48
        myoglobin, 48
    magnesium, 41, 42, 46, 47
    phosphorus, 41, 42, 46
    potassium, 41, 47, 48, 51, 105, 106
Mint, 60, 71, 93
Montaigne, 55

♣ N ♣

Nasturtiums, 62
National Academy of Sciences, *Diet, Nutrition and Cancer*, 28
Nucleic acids, DNA & RNA, 46

♣ P ♣

PAH, polycyclic aromatic hydrocarbons, 30
Peanut Butter & Cabbage Snack, 73
Pearson, Durk and Sandy Shaw, *Life Extension: A Practical Scientific Approach,* 29
Pennyroyal, 61, 64
Pepsin, 36, 45, 69
Philistion, 23, 95, 103
Pineapple, 71, 75, 76, 90
Piñon nuts, 77, 78, 85
Plain Ol' Sauerkraut, 83
Plath, Sylvia, "Who," *Crossing the Water,* 69

Pliny the Elder, 23, 50, 108, *Natural History,* 23
Poppy seeds, 71
Prevention of illness, 24, 25, 28, 30, **33,** 97
Pyrethrum, 67
Pythagoras, 23

♣ R ♣

Rabelais, 49
Rhazes, 27
Rhubarb, 39, 61
Riley, James Whitcomb, 16, 17, "Bud's Fairy Tale," 17
RNA—see Nucleic acids
Roman Empire, 26, Romans 12, 13, 22-24, 30, 95
Rosemary, 61
Rousseau, Jean-Jacques, 57, 58
Rue, 62, 102
Russia, 39, 84; Russian, 26, 39, 112

♣ S ♣

Sage, 61, 71, 93, 108
Sarah Orne Jewett, 40
Sauerkraut, 32, 35, 48, 53, 82, 83, 87, 91, 97-99, 103, 105, 106, 107, 110
    juice, 32, 35, 83, 91, 97, 105
Scotland, 29, 57, 60; Findhorn, 57
Shive, Dr. William, 36
Slugs—see Gardening, pests
Snails—see Gardening, pests
Sorrel, 71
Southernwood, 61
Strawberries, 62
Sunflower seeds, 71
Sweet & Sour Cole Slaw, 75

♣ T ♣

Theophrastus, *Inquiry Into Plants,* 22

Thuricide—see *Bacillus thuringiensis*
(B.t.)
Thyme, 60, 93
Thyroid, 43, 102, deficiencies, 43
Tomatoes, 60, 62, 64, 73
Turkey, 22

♣ V ♣
Valjean, Dr., 95, 110
Vitamins, 19, 29, **41-45**, 82, 90,
91, 94
ascorbic acid, 44
bioflavonoids, 41, 42, 44
citrin, 44
hesperidin, 44
quercetin, 44
rutin, 44
fat-soluble, 43, 45
retinol equivalents, (IU) 43, 44
supplements, 29, 42

vitamin A, 41, 43
vitamin B-6 (pyridoxine), 41,
42, **44**
vitamin C, 38, 40-42, **44-45**,
68, 69, 83, 91, 99, 101, 105,
110, 113
vitamin K, 41, **45**, 96, 107
vitamin P, 44
vitamin U, 36, 41, **45**, 69, 105,
112
water-soluble, 43, 44, 69
Voltaire, 38

♣ W ♣
Webworms—see Gardening, pests
White, Hellebore, 67

♣ Y ♣
Yugoslavia, 22

❖❖❖❖❖❖❖❖❖❖❖❖❖❖❖❖❖

*"Nobody ever expected me
to be President. In my poor,
lean, lank face nobody has
ever seen that any cabbages
were sprouting out."*
—*Abraham Lincoln*

❖❖❖❖❖❖❖❖❖❖❖❖❖❖❖